Wild Bill Hickok

and the

Wrath of the Dead Rabbits

James Mic Regan

Wild Bill Hickok and the Wrath of the Dead Rabbits
by James Mic Regan

Signalman Publishing   2012
www.signalmanpublishing.com
email: info@signalmanpublishing.com
Kissimmee, Florida

Cover design by Peggy Ann Rupp, DBS Design

ISBN: 978-1-935991-32-8 (paperback)
        978-1-935991-33-5 (ebook)

Library of Congress Control Number: 2011940178

Signalman
Publishing

In Memory of

My grandfather on my mother's side, Elmer Lucas

and

*My brother, Thomas John Regan, who had travelled with me as I conducted the research for this book. Tommy was a true Irishman and real **PARD**. Tommy passed away August 2, 1996, 120 years to the day of the murder of Wild Bill Hickok.*

TABLE OF CONTENTS

Introduction vii

One: Deadman's Hand 1

Two: Kidd Kelly 5

Three: Gangsters 12

Four: Dead Rabbitswest..22

Five: It's a Circus in Hays...26

Six: Shoot The Hound...44

Seven: He Ain't No School Kid..51

Eight: Along Comes Jack...61

Nine: Annihilation...65

Ten: Operation Duck Bill...74

Eleven: Set 'Im Up..82

Twelve: Plug Uglies..96

Thirteen: Don't Let Your Tongue Cut Yourthroat.................100

Fourteen: Den of The Dead Rabbits 104

Fifteen: Lips Now Sealed.. 111

Sixteen: In The Spirit of Littlemary 113

Seventeen: Dodge City Dandys 116

Eighteen: A Storm Begins to Blow 123

Nineteen: A Dog Pack Splits...127

Twenty: Road Kill...136

Twenty One: Custer's Gold..141

Twenty Two: The Morgue...144

Twenty Three: Ghost Dance 149

Twenty Four: Full Fledged Whyos 167

The Author's Research...174

Acknowledgements...193

Deadwood Daze..195

INTRODUCTION

James Butler "Wild Bill" Hickok, an American Old West character, Union Civil War veteran, hunting guide, Army courier, gambler, gunfighter, lawman, etc. Some considered Wild Bill to be the quickest, most accurate and deadliest gunman of his era. His exploits and "tales" were written up in Eastern dime novel magazines with estimates of 10 to 100 total man kills. Wild Bill was dubbed "Prince of the Pistoleers".

James Butler Hickok was born on May 27, 1837 in Troy Grove, Illinois. He grew up to be a tall, slim man, sporting long hair with a well-groomed mustache. After fighting for the Union in the U.S. Civil War, Hickok did a short time as a courier with the 7th Cavalry.

Wild Bill became the Marshal of Hays City, Kansas in 1869 at the same time that Lieutenant Colonel George Custer and the 7th Cavalry were stationed at Fort Hays. While the lawman of Hays, Hickok got into gunfights with two civilians, killing both. In 1870 Wild Bill got into a bar fight with two soldiers of the 7th Cavalry, killing one and wounding the other.

In 1871, Hickok became the Marshal of Abilene, Kansas. He shot and killed a gambler in a gunfight but also shot to death his own deputy. Wild Bill joined Buffalo Bill's Wild West Show for a while and then got married in 1876. In July of 1876, Hickok and his "only trusted friend", California Joe, showed up in Deadwood, Dakota Territory to join in on the Gold Rush.

On the afternoon of August 2, 1876, in the Number Ten Saloon of Deadwood, Wild Bill was shot in the back and killed while playing cards. The cards that Hickok held were a pair of aces, and a pair of eights— forever known as the "Deadman's Hand". A man named Jack McCall was charged with the murder and found innocent, in Deadwood. However, he was re-arrested, re-tried and hung for the murder of Wild Bill in Yankton, Dakota Territory in 1877.

These facts can be found in history books and are well documented in Joseph G. Rosa's book, *They Called Him Wild Bill*.

However, there are many questions that are unanswered and mysteries left unsolved to this day on the assassination of Wild Bill Hickok.

Why did "Colorado" Charlie Utter, the self-proclaimed, *Pard* of Wild Bill, escort Hickok to the Number Ten Saloon on August 2, 1876 and then leave him moments before he was assassinated?

Why would Jack McCall use the excuse that he shot Wild Bill because Hickok had killed his brother, when McCall never had a brother?

How did the card player sitting across from Wild Bill get shot?

How did Jack McCall, a known vagrant about Deadwood, become a well-dressed man with money to burn the day after his first trial?

Why was Jack McCall denied his civil right of "No Double Jeopardy" when he was retried for a crime he had already been found innocent for, by a jury of his peers and against the wishes of Governor Pennington who wanted McCall pardoned?

What was Jack McCall attempting to talk about just before he was hung, when he wrote to two newspapers, offering up "The Plot To Kill Wild Bill"?

Who gunned down Wild Bill's trusted friend, California Joe, and why, in a U.S. Army fort, within two months of Hickok being killed?

Why did undertaker Doc Ellis Pierce wait until 1925 to state that along with the bullet wound that killed Wild Bill, he also found knife wounds on Wild Bill's body?

Why did Peter LeFlemme wait until 1949 to state to a newspaper his version of what he saw when Wild Bill Hickok was killed?

Was it just a coincidence that the murder scene was burnt to the ground, causing confusion in what transpired when Wild Bill was killed?

How did Jack McCall come into possession of a U.S. Army pistol when he was never in the Army?

It is: 'THE SMOKIN' GUN'

A .22-caliber pistol taken from Jack McCall, who shot and killed Wild Bill Hickok in Deadwood, South Dakota. The weapon was found on McCall after he had been arrested the second time. A miners' jury had acquitted him in Deadwood. The government did not recognize the verdict because the trial had taken place on Indian land. The weapon was owned by Sergeant Theodore Benson, Company C, Fifth Regiment, at Fort Fetterman, who may have been a member of the patrol which arrested McCall. Benson was discharged three days before Custer left for Little Big Horn. Courtesy Wyoming State Archives and Historical Department.

For 130 years, no one has come forward to answer the questions, solve the mysteries or offer up any good theories to why Jack McCall would want to kill Wild Bill Hickok…

UNTIL NOW!

In the era just before the Civil War a gang of young Irish Hooligans roamed the lower East Side of New York City. Their battle flag, when going to war against other gangs, was a dead rabbit impaled on a spear.

THEIR MOTTO:

"DEATH TO THOSE WHO TREAD ON US"

THE WRATH OF THE DEAD RABBITS

Stories supported by historical data and statements seem to suggest that an Irish clan of Kelly's, who came to the United States of America from Ireland, organized the Dead Rabbits Gang of muggerines, pickpocketers, thugaloons, strong-arm robbers and killers in New York City circa 1850. They obtained their trade name due to their custom of leaving dead rabbits on rival gang member's corpses.

Many gang members joined the Northern Union Army during the U.S. Civil War, being incorporated into the all-Irish regiment, the New York Fighting 69th.

They became members of the all-Irish dreaded "WHYOS" gang of New York City after the U.S. Civil War. They were the most vicious gang of hit men that terrorized the lower East Side for some 40 years, with gang members sashaying about the city, carrying their victim's eyeballs in their vest pockets.

Many enlisted in George Custer's 7th Cavalry, U.S. Army after the Civil War. They initiated the "Irish Avengers" and eventually the "Custer's Avengers" after the battle of Little Big Horn.

They persuaded the Custer Avengers to hire an Indian tracker, the deadliest cannibalistic Indian killer known to the U.S. Army as "Liver Eater". He had waged a 20-year one-man vendetta against the Crow Indian Nation to avenge the killing and mutilation of his pregnant wife. He was dubbed "Absaroka Dapiek" and got credit for some 300 Indian organs passing through his gullet.

They plotted, carried out and covered up the assassinations of Wild Bill Hickok in Deadwood, South Dakota, and his only trusted friend, California Joe. When Joe made the catastrophic decision to enter the Den of the Dead Rabbits in Ft. Robinson, Nebraska he was to never return. All of this was in retaliation for Hickok slaying fellow Irish clansmen and 7th Cavalry soldier, John Kelly.

They silenced Jack McCall, the man charged with the killing of Hickok, by having him re-arrested for the murder and hung when McCall foolishly attempted to blackmail the gang. The Irish gang had gotten McCall cleared at his first trial and paid him off handsomely for his part in the plot to kill Hickok. However, McCall failed to adhere to an Irish proverb, "Don't let your tongue cut your throat."

They broke the neck of the greatest Oglala Sioux Indian warrior to ever live, Chief Crazy Horse, to finish him off, after he had been lanced by a U.S. Army soldier. This was to fulfill an old Irish curse to the enemy: "To tread on the smallest member of our clan will cause for the destruction of your greatest!" (An Oglala Sioux had scalped "alive" five year-old Mary Kelly).

They joined the "Dog Kelley Gang" of Dodge City, Kansas, from 1877 to1881, with Bat, Ed and Jim Masterson, Wyatt and Virgil Earp, Doc

Holliday and other top western gunman of that era. The gang operated saloons, gambling halls and prostitution cribs.

They returned to Deadwood in the year 1879 to pay a visit to Charlie Storm who had threatened to publish an account that a gang of Irish soldiers were behind the murder of Wild Bill Hickok. The Kelly's did not locate Storm, but to eliminate the evidence of the murder scene, the Irish gangsters baked a loaf of bread in the local bakery that turned the town of Deadwood in to TOAST.

They had the luck of the Irish when Charlie Storm blew into Tombstone, Arizona and boasted that with Wild Bill Hickok dead, he was the new "Prince of the Pistoleers". Storm was soon rendered Tombstone road kill.

They ran with the notorious William Bonney "Billy the Kid" gang of New Mexico, circa 1881.

They ignited the fuse to obliterate the Sioux Indian Nation in December of 1890, to take final vengeance for Little Big Horn. The Custer Avengers saw to the execution of Chief Sitting Bull and the shooting down of Bull's son, Crowfoot. They then rioted the 7th Cavalry into releasing the "Red Dog Reapers" on Sioux men, women and children at Wounded Knee, South Dakota.

"Let's give the Sioux a bloody Merry Christmas and let the snow bury 'em."

They gunned down Bob Ford, the back-shooting killer of Jesse James, in Creede, Colorado, June 1892, to fulfill a decree set down to become a full-fledged Irish WHYOS. "A guy ain't tough until he has knocked his man out!"

These stories are all about different versions of demises of these American Old West characters, different from any version written to date.

These are stories my Grandfather told me, in the late 1950s and early 1960s, when I was a teenager. These same stories were passed to my Grandfather from another character right out of the Old West. This character divulged to my Grandfather that he was one of an Irish clan of Kelly's, who belonged to Irish gangs of New York City, the all-Irish U.S. Union Army Regiment, New York's "Fighting 69th" and George Custer's 7th Cavalry.

I never intended to write a book on these other versions, for I was no author and had to spend my time making a living. But these many years later

I happened upon much documented material that strongly corroborated Grandpa's retold stories. I knew that I had to make some sort of an attempt to record these other versions, no matter how long it took me. Someone else out there had to be interested in at least hearing them. I may be the only person left able or willing to tell them.

The convincing shot to me was when I saw George Custer's 7th Cavalry muster roll call. These names stood out like green shamrocks in a field of white cotton:
Kelley, James: Trumpeter, Company B;
Kelly, John: Private, Company F;
Kelly, George: Private, Company H;
Kelly, James: Private, Company H;
Kelly, Patrick: Private, Company I.

"Why there's more Kelly's than Custer's, (George, Tom and Boston), in the 7th Cavalry!"

That did it! So I took those stories my Grandpa repeated to me and with the documented facts to support them, (in fact, more evidence than there is to support any other version), I went on to Montreal, Wisconsin, to my sister Carole's summer home, to write this book.

So, if you are a reading fan of the American Old West, or if you just crave a good mystery of assassinations, murder, conspiracies, betrayal, government cover-ups, secret sects, street gangs, massacres and complete revenge, your curiosity will force you to read on.

On the other hand, if you desire a little romance, Scottish knight chivalry, a bit of a dog story, guns and knives, circus trick shooting, the sport of pugilism or arm wrestling, the game of billiards, to eat donuts or consume liver, to play and gamble at cards, to drink intoxicants, to smoke tobacco, to wear tattoos, to patronize, live with, or be the wild and woolliest woman and to ride Harley's: **There is something too in this book for you!!**

But foremost, if you are Irish, especially one with the last name of Kelly or Kelley, this is required reading to obtain a degree in your ethnic rootsology.

Now read on and learn why, no matter how hard you try and although it is quite possible to train a live one.

YOU CAN'T TAME
A DEAD RABBIT

CHAPTER ONE
DEADMAN'S HAND

The stories my Grandfather told me concerning a Kidd Kelly all started over a card game we had been playing one night at my family's home in Hillside, Illinois.It was on one of his visits during my high school years of 1958 to 1962.

My Grandpa and I were playing a game of draw poker and it was a rare occasion this night because it was one time when I was lucky enough to be winning, playing against him. Grandpa carried with him a large set of wooden nickels to use for poker chips. I was raking in the chips with my poker hand of 2 black Aces and 2 black eights, to his pair of Kings. That got Grandpa going.

"Well, Jimmy," he started, "your luck is about to run out. Do you know what you are holding?"

"Sure," I answered smartly, trying to impress my Grandpa with my knowledge of the American Old West. "Deadman's hand, the same two pair of cards Wild Bill Hickok was holding when he was shot in the back and killed while playing cards in the Number Ten Saloon of Deadwood, South Dakota, on August 2, 1876."

"Good," Grandpa snapped, "but what was the fifth card?"

"I don't think anybody really knows," I came back with. "Some say a Jack, others say a Queen."

"No one does know," Grandpa continued. "Ya see, Hickok was holding his five cards in his right hand. The top card, or the fifth, was stacked over the other four and right under Hickok's right thumb. The bullet that hit Hickok went through the back of his neck and out the right side of his face. When the bullet came out it threw blood over Hickok's right hand, completely covering the top card. It seems no one later cared to wipe Hickok's blood and flesh off the top card."

"Yea, I can see how that could happen," I replied.

"And it wasn't two black Aces and two black Eights like most people think," Grandpa went on. "In the Old West the four suits of cards were four separate colors for easy identification. Hearts were red, Diamonds blue, Clubs green and Spades black. Now do you know who killed Hickok, and why, Jimmy?"

"Yea, some drifter named Jack McCall," I said. "Said he shot Hickok because Hickok killed his brother."

"Wrong," Grandpa asserted. "Jack McCall had no brothers. Only sisters. McCall got that excuse from a U.S. Army soldier that was kin to another soldier that Hickok had gunned down. Both the soldiers were part of a gang that set McCall up to take the rap. Why, the idiot McCall didn't even have a loaded gun!"

"Didn't have a loaded gun!" I was chuckling as I spoke. "Come on, Grandpa, Hickok didn't shoot himself."

"It's no damn joke, Jimmy!" Grandpa flared back. "Hickok was shot by one of the two U.S. Army soldiers that were behind McCall and shot at the same time that McCall supposedly fired his revolver. One soldier missed Hickok and accidentally shot the card player across from Hickok."

"But, Grandpa," I then said, and acted serious so he didn't suspect me thinking he was telling some yarn. "The witnesses that were there in the Number Ten Saloon when Hickok was shot never mentioned anything about seeing anyone else shooting or even anybody else besides McCall with a gun in hand."

"Jimmy," Grandpa continued in a demeanor less perturbed. "The reason no one in the Number Ten saw anyone with a revolver in hand is simple. The out of uniform Irish soldiers who shot Hickok and the card player across the table, were not in the Number Ten."

"Man," I finally cut in. "You've got me all confused now, Grandpa."

"You're not the only one," Grandpa continued. "You see, there was a dance hall next door to the Number Ten Saloon and there was an open archway in the wall that connected the two establishments. It was this archway that Wild Bill had his back to while sitting at the card table and not the front or back door of the saloon. That most think. Two assassins were shooting through this archway, from the dance hall that was not in use and dark during daytime hours. The reason why ninety nine percent of Wild Bill Hickok murder sleuths never took this archway into consideration of the murder scene is because these Irish gangsters burnt down the entire city block that housed the Number Ten Saloon and the next door dance hall."

"Grandpa," I then said. "How come you know all this? And why would the U.S. Army want to kill Wild Bill?"

"Hickok had gunned down an unarmed soldier who had received the Medal of Honor," he answered. "Go make us some Cowboy Coffee. It's going to be a long night. You do know how to make Cowboy Coffee, don't you Jimmy?"

"Yea sure," I said. "Boil a pot of water, toss in some coffee grounds, slowly count to sixty, then remove the pot from the fire to let the grounds settle. But this ain't Deadwood, Grandpa. We got electricity and a percolator!"

I was always interested in reading or hearing about any Old West story and this one sounded like a dandy. It had also been a rare occasion for me to be winning at poker against Grandpa and I didn't care much about playing on just to be jinxed by the:

"DEADMAN'S HAND."

CHAPTER TWO
KIDD KELLY

My Grandfather on my mother's side, Elmer Lucas, had been in the United States Army during World War I. Once the war was over and he was honorably discharged, Elmer traveled about the western territory of the U.S. looking for employment.

The year is about 1920 and Elmer is in his 20's. He has found a job as a bartender on Whiskey Row in Prescott, Arizona. One day Elmer goes to the Fort Whipple Army Hospital of Prescott to receive medical treatment for a bad lung infection. As all servicemen do to one another, he easily strikes up a conversation with a strange looking elderly veteran.

It is now summer time and this old veteran is dressed in a t-shirt and Levi pants with one of the pant legs cut at the knee to expose a wooden peg leg. Strapped to this man's belt is an old flapped U.S. Army holster with revolver. The man is tall and lean with long gray hair pulled back in a ponytail, to match his gray goatee. Elmer shakes hands with this old veteran and notices a strange tattoo on the man's right forearm. It is a human skull over crossed cavalry sabers painted in black. Jutting out a jagged hole in the top of the skull is a green colored number seven.

This veteran introduces himself as Kidd Kelly and Elmer immediately thinks to himself that this has got to be the oldest "KID" he has ever met. Elmer and Kidd strike up a conversation, but the only thing that Elmer learns this day, about this old timer, is that he lost the lower half of his right leg from gangrene setting into an old war wound.

Elmer figures that the name Kidd is just some sort of nickname. But Elmer knows that in the Old West it is good sense *not* to pry into another's identity or past. And this state of Arizona, which recently joined the union as the 48th state, has the reputation of a *Desperado* haven. But Elmer feels comfortable in this Old West character's company even though there is about a 60-year age difference. Elmer invites Kidd to stop off at the Bird Cage Saloon on Whiskey Row and "I'll buy ya a shot and beer".

Within several days, Kidd Kelly takes Elmer up on the offer and stops in the Bird Cage during Elmer's working hours. Kidd is still in his same clothes and Elmer detects that Kidd may have been sleeping out and in need of a bath. Kidd is wearing his revolver and although there is no law in Arizona against wearing side arms, it is unlawful to wear one in this saloon.

Before Elmer can serve Kidd a shot and beer, he requests to hold Kidd's weapon behind the bar. Kidd at first hesitates, but trusting Elmer, he hands over his piece. Elmer can see that it is an old Colt single action .45 caliber Peacemaker. On the barrel of the pistol is an engraving that reads *Fear no enemy of any size, Just call on me and I'll equalize.* "That's some quote on your pistol, Kidd," Elmer comments.

Elmer is just ending his tour as bartender, so he invites the Kidd to drink with him at the bar. Elmer, knowing that Kelly is Irish, orders a bottle of the saloon's premier stock of Irish whiskey.

Kidd comments, "Do you know why whiskey bottles are made with a narrow neck, Elmer? So an Irishman won't empty the bottle in one swig." Elmer chuckles as these two 'ole vets' empty the contents of the whiskey bottle in an equally divided dozen swigs.

Kidd's Irish tongue is now loose, causing much wagging to start, just as two large men with looks of Indian sit down at the bar several stools over from Kidd.

Kidd cracks to Elmer, "Ya serve Indians in here, do ya?"

"We're Bible totin' people," Elmer answers. Jesus himself said, "It's not what goes in your mouth that counts, but what comes out."

"Well, Elmer," Kidd returns. "We'll see what comes out after they slop down a few whiskeys." Kidd continues on, "Ya know, Elmer, I came to this here Bird Cage Saloon years ago to visit a young niece a mine, called Katheran 'Canary Kate' Kelly. She used to sing and swing in a large bird cage that was lowered down through a hole in the ceiling from the second floor. The soldiers, miners and gamblers would throw money into the cage to get her to show off her canary tattoos that she wore on her hips. A yellow canary on one side, a green one on the other.

Kidd puts his right arm on the bar, palm up, as Elmer orders two beers to wash the whiskey taste down their throats. "See this tattoo, Elmer?" The Kidd says, showing the skull, sabers and number seven on his forearm. "The seven is for the 7th Cavalry."

"Custer's 7th?" Elmer says.

"Yea," Kidd answers. "Lieutenant Colonel George Armstrong Custer. George was one of the youngest Generals in the Civil War, but his rank was reduced for the reconstructed U.S. Army after the war, as other Generals. Did you know, Elmer, that George's brother Tom was a twice receiver of the Congressional Medal of Honor in the Civil War?"

"No I didn't," Elmer answers.

"Yea I knew them both well," Kidd says. "I was in the 7th, but I was doing intelligence and operated on my own. I was blessed with 'The Luck of the Irish' when I didn't go to Little Big Horn with the Custer's."

One of the Indians who was sitting and drinking, three stools down from the Kidd, now comments aloud for all the saloon to hear, "Too bad George Custer and his brothers got their asses blown away by the Sioux Indians at Little Big Horn."

"Well look what's come outta his mouth," Kidd states louder. "And who the hell are you, to be hornin' in on our conversation?" Kidd growls.

"I am a full blood Yavapai Indian of Arizona," the Redman answers. "But all us Indians are brothers."

"Well bro, maybe so," Kidd comes back. "But your brothers didn't get ALL of my 7th Cavalry brothers at Little Big Horn. The rest of us returned the favor. We snapped the neck of Crazy Horse. Had Sitting Bull and his son gunned-down. And then we mowed down your red dog buddies at Wounded Knee and dumped 'em in a trash pit. What ya got to squeal to that?" Kidd crackles in come-back-piss'em-off-ism.

This crack by the Kidd gets the Indian's booze-laden blood a-rollin, so the red man reacts by standing up from his stool while pulling a knife from his boot. The Kidd reflexes by standing up himself and reaching to his old army holster for the Colt .45 that is no longer there.

Before these two warriors can joust, the female bartender who had replaced Elmer behind the bar fires off a gun shot into the roof with Kidd's old Colt that Elmer had lodged behind the bar. "If there's goin' to be any killin' in here today, I'll be a-doin' it!" the girl forcibly snaps. "It's high time ya all take your Little Big Horn elsewhere."

The man who had come into the Bird Cage with the Indian, now grabs the enraged Indian by the arm to hustle him out the front door. As the two exit, Kidd Kelly hollers, "You should get on your knees and thank God you're still on your feet cause if I'd a had my pistol, as sure as you're a Redman, you'd be a Deadman!"

"Elmer," the bartendress snaps! "You need to take your friend outta here now. I'll hold his revolver until tomorrow."

"Let's go to my place, Kidd," Elmer suggests. "I've got plenty there for us to drink."

Elmer's apartment is just three doors down and one floor up from the Bird Cage. Once there, Elmer pours two drinks and invites Kidd to unwind in the confines of his hot water deep bath tub.

Kidd, in dire need of a good scrub down, accepts the offer. Once well waterlogged, the Kidd steps out from the bathroom with a towel wrapped around his waist. Elmer sees that the Kidd not only has the tattoo of skull over sabers on his right forearm, but three more to go with it. On Kidd's left forearm is the word 'WHYOS'. Left upper arm has a rabbit impaled on a spear. Right upper arm has a tattoo of a double KK.

"You're looking like a sailor right off a pirate ship," Elmer says as he hands Kidd a fresh change of clothes to borrow. But drawing no comment from the tuff looking old character adds, "You're welcome to stay the night or two on my couch."

"I'm beholden to you, Elmer," Kidd states while dressing. "If you hadn't of taken my Colt, I'd a killed that Indian for pulling a knife on me. Most likely I'd be staying the night and maybe many more in the Prescott jail."

Kidd relaxes on the couch as Elmer tosses some wood into a pot belly stove, leaving the metal door open. Summer days are quite warm in Prescott, but nights can get quite nippy in the mile high Prescott Mountains. The monsoon season is at full blast this night. But it won't be the rain that keeps these two Army vets up all night. Elmer knows that Kidd is too wound up from the excitement at the Bird Cage, and there is a good supply of yapping medicine available in Elmer's liquor cabinet. Elmer sits at his eating table, pulls out a can of tobacco and some small fine paper, to roll a few cigarettes for himself and Kidd.

"Forget all that hassle, Elmer," Kidd says. "Go on down to my Ford Model-T that's parked out front the Cage and get my old Army saddle bag that's on the floor board. I got some nice smokin' pipes and fine tobacco."

Elmer goes for the saddle bag and returns in minutes.

Kidd reaches in to draw out two pipes and a brown rawhide pouch. He tosses the pouch to Elmer while commenting, "You'll like this cherry flavored stuff, Elmer."

Elmer, while packing his pipe, notices that the pouch is made of fine Indian embroidered rawhide bearing the initials J.B.H.

"J.B.H.?" Elmer asks.

"James Butler Hickok," Kidd answers.

"Wild Bill Hickok?" Elmer questions again?

Kidd doesn't answer. Instead he stares into the fire of the pot belly stove, while puffing his pipe. After many seconds Kidd responds, "Elmer, the double KK tattoo I wear is for my kin, the Kelly clan. Wild Bill Hickok gunned down one of the clan so some of us knocked 'im out. The rabbit on the spear tattoo is for an Irish gang we formed as teenagers on the streets of New York City, in order to survive. The WHYOS is an Irish gang I joined in New York after I ran around Dodge City, Kansas, with the Dog Kelley Gang."

"Dodge City, Kansas, eh?" Elmer questions. "Did you ever meet the Earp's?"

"Sure." Kidd responds. "Met 'em in Dodge. They were in the Dogs Gang. Was with 'em in Tombstone, Arizona, and ran into Wyatt and his brother Virgil in a town called Tonopah, Nevada. Virgil became a deputy sheriff in the adjacent town of Goldfield, even though he swore under oath that he was never involved in a 'gun duel'. I guess Goldfield never heard of the OK Corral. Wyatt tried to open up a brothel but his wife 'pulled up the reins on that one'."

"I didn't know Wyatt Earp was involved with prostitutes." Elmer questions. "I thought they were the good guys?"

"Good guys!" Kidd snaps. "There were no good guys when it came to gunfighters. Wyatt Earp was arrested several times in Peoria, Illinois, for being a pimp before he became a lawman and was known as the 'Peoria Bummer'. Why, Ben Thompson gunned down so many men it made him eligible to be a lawman! There was no such thing as a fair gunfight in the West or anywhere else. Most were shot in the back, ambushed or bushwhacked. Sit back and relax, Elmer." Kidd rambles on…

"Enjoy the pipe. We'll sip some whiskey and I'll fill ya in on some REAL history of the Irish and the 7th Cavalry."

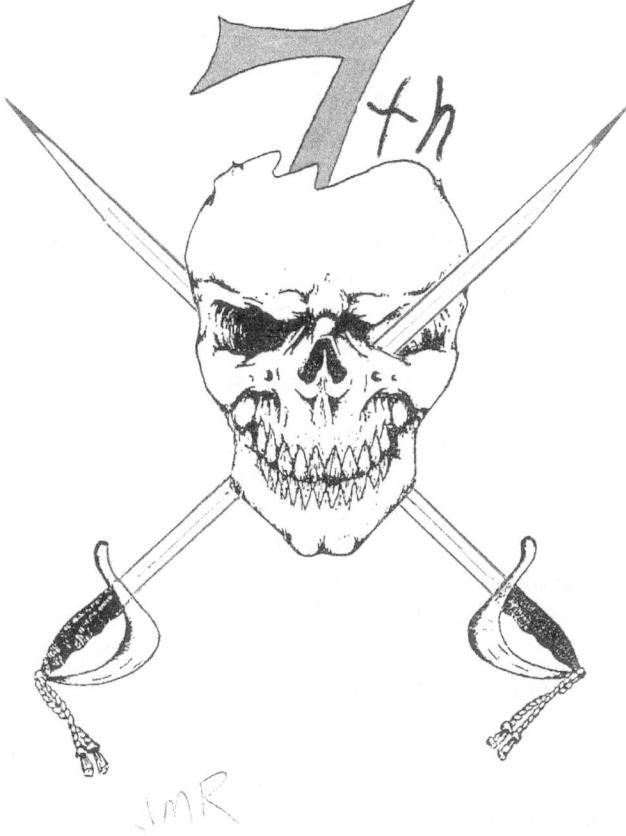

CHAPTER THREE
GANGSTERS

1845 to 1850 sees the country of Ireland engulfed in a black plague that devastates the farmer's potato crop. So many of the Irish had relied on the potato for their entire means of survival that one million of Ireland's population will die of starvation, or the diseases brought on before the plague runs its course. Many adults just walk away from their families to leave what food for the young and are never seen again. Most farmers that do survive lose their farms to the English landowners or carpetbaggers causing hatred between Irish and English that will last for centuries. Some of the luckier Irish are able to survive by obtaining enough funds to flee their homeland for the western world of America. Englishmen buy the Irish passage tickets in order to get the Irish off their land.

The worst year of the pestilence is Black '47, with many more Irish perishing on the ships during the trip to the United States. Bodies are thrown to the sharks to halt any spread of disease. The boats are christened *coffin ships*. The Irish Immigrants do not have a choice in where they set ashore in the New World. But it does not matter as long as they get somewhere and off those coffin ships. Some Irish come ashore in the Northern U.S. port of New York City, some at the Southern port of New Orleans, Louisiana and others into the country of Canada.

The year 1850 sees a clan of Irish with the last names of Kelly; brothers, sisters, parents, aunts, uncles and cousins make their new homes in the Lower East Side of New York City, with other Irish families. Because the Kelly's don't all come to the New World at once and may speak an Irish Brogue of broken English, the U.S. Immigration authorities spell the Kelly name on the immigrations papers, the way they hear it: Kelly, Kelley, O'Kelley, Killey or Kile.

The majority of these Kelly's that have landed in New York are young, with many of the adults in Ireland only having enough funds to send their children over, or having died from starvation for saving what food for their offspring. The majority of the oldest of the young Kelly's are female with one strong-willed female of stout character taking the helm of the clan:Kolleen Kelly.Kolleen, with younger brother, Jack, make the commitment to do what is necessary to hold together the Kelly clan. Kolleen and Jack together are also in charge of raising their adolescent younger brother whom they call "Kidd". Kolleen, Jack and Kidd's father had disappeared in Ireland during the potato plague and rumor has it that the father had wandered off to die, so to leave what food for the children. The three Kelly's remember their father's last words:

"THE ADULT MUST GIVE THE SUPREME SACRIFICE TO INSURE THAT THE KELLY BLOOD LINE CARRIES ON".

Their mother is still in Ireland due to money being short, but intentions are for her to come across on a later date.

Now jobs are scarce for the Irish Immigrants in New York City. The Irish are considered by other residents as, "low class and white trash". Business establishments that have hung out Help Wanted signs also have billings posted that read:

"IRISH NEED NOT APPLY".

The Irish women are more fortunate than the men and girls of the Kelly clan being able to procure hard work from the rich of the city through the efforts of local Catholic Churches. Some obtain barmaid roles at the neighborhood saloons, and some desperate Irish girls take to the streets as prostitutes.

Jack Kelly has no desire to sit idle while the Kelly girls forage about the city to support the clan. He will do what had to be done in Ireland when the potato ran out. Go on the hunt. Jack has noticed that there are several well-wooded city parks in New York City that make homes for small game animals of rabbit, squirrel and pheasants. With the aid of an Irish buddy, Bill Gentles, and younger brother Kidd, Jack forms a gang of Irish youths to take up the craft of hunting small game animals.

Billy Gentles has the ability to design and manufacture well-balanced sharp wooden spears made from tree branches. Gentles' teaches the young Irish boys how to chuck the spears at the game animals in the city parks. For his expertise, Bill Gentles earns the tag "Lance".

But young Irish females of New York City are not going to be left out of the action. An ambitious young female "tomboy" named Katherine Shannahan whose father was one of the rare countrymen of Ireland, who made a living fishing the sea rather than farming potatoes, makes nets of thin rope, like her Dad had taught her, to "fish" for game by tossing the nets at animals on the run or down on them from her position in the trees. Katherine teaches other Irish girls her art. Obtaining her nickname "Snags", Shannahan and her female gang are known as "The Snaggers".

But not all Irish youths are capable of having the ability to chuck spears, or snag small game with nets. Young Tommy O'Ryan has his own unique tactic to gather up prey for the hunt. Tommy, who loves to play with matches, uses a recipe of explosive black gun powder and flammable pine turpentine in a mixture, to lob into the den tunnels of rabbits and squirrels, so to blast and drive out the animals through their secondary holes and into the awaiting hands of the gang's spear chuckers and snaggers. O'Ryan, with his explosive incendiary devices that he calls "Tommy bombs", inherits the dub "Tommy the Turp" (Turpentine). Some call O'Ryan "Pyro Tommy" for his pyromania. But it is a handle that none dare call to Tommy's face. The Turp's technique is very effective, but in a short time the terrain of the city parks will look like the surface of the moon, with more craters than a block of Swiss cheese.

The Irish gang of young hunters become quite prolific at their craft. Making for much meat to settle into the kitchen kettles of the poor Irish immigrants in New York City's Lower East Side. The Irish girls make necklaces of rabbit feet and decorate themselves and their hair with pretties of pheasant or other bird feathers.

Initially it is only a half-hearted effort by the local city police, for the first several years, to catch the young Irish small group game hunters that roam the city parks. And because they see the Irish youths running through the city parks with rabbits impaled on their hunting spears, it is the cops who call them "Those damn' Dead Rabbits Kids".

But as the young hoolligans grow older, the pursuit by the cops will go on to a higher level when the Dead Rabbits Gang pursues bigger game.

In the year 1856, the Kelly's of Jack, Kolleen and Kidd receive word from their relatives across the ocean in Ireland, that their mother will not be leaving the homeland to join them in America. Their mother has died from a fever and young Kidd Kelly will never forget the Irish proverb that sister Kolleen quotes when he questions why their mother did not receive any treatment from the English-owned hospital near her home: **"Death is a poor man's doctor."**

These words stick hard in the 15 year-old Kidd's mind as he vows to himself that the Kelly clan will never again not have the funds to afford the service of a doctor. "If the Irish can not get the jobs that are graced to other ethnic groups of New York City, then we will sweep clean the purses of those who get!"

Kidd Kelly takes over the leadership of the teenage Dead Rabbits Gang from older brother Jack, who has decided to join the Catholic Priesthood even though he has fathered a son with a local Irish prostitute. Jack does not marry the girl, but allows her to give the boy the Kelly name. The baby boy is christened Jack Kelly Junior.

With Kidd Kelly now at the helm, the Dead Rabbit Gang graduates from small game hunting in the city parks to pick-pocketing, mugging and strong-arm robbing human game in the alleys and on the streets of the Lower East Side of New York City. In order to take on these new careers about the city, the Irish gang must move in on another long established gang that already patrols the streets and alleys of the Lower East Side. As all gang life goes, whether it be made up of young or old, times will eventually turn deadly—especially if other gangs are lurking about and very especially if the other gang is made up of the hated English.

A gang of thugs known as the "Bowery's" whom the Dead Rabbits call "The Limey's", control most of the Lower East Side and they consider themselves the "Homeboys", with the Irish being outside immigrant trash. The Dead Rabbits venture into territory the Limey's believe belongs to them. So, no doubt a confrontation takes order in the middle of Paradise Square at the Five Points Intersection in the Lower East Side of New York City.

Young Kidd Kelly at the head of his all-Irish gang faces off with the leader of the Limeys. An argument begins over the Dead Rabbits "belonging in the woods and not on the streets", a crack by the Limey that causes Kidd to throw the first punch and knock the English lad to the ground. But Kidd Kelly has brought his fist to a gunfight (at that time, a gun was a weapon that the Dead Rabbits have not yet utilized). The Limey's leader arises from the ground the Kidd had put him to, with a pistol in hand. As the English youth cocks his old single shot black powder Flintlock, with dead aim on Kidd Kelly, a fishing net is thrown from out of the crowd of Dead Rabbits and from the hands of the lass, Snags Shannahan. Her net is followed by a wooden spear from the hands of Lance Gentles. The spear still has a bloody rabbit impaled on it! Snags' skillfully thrown net traps and freezes the Limey in his position. Lance's accurately thrown spear torpedoes his chest to immediately take him down. As the mortally wounded Limey hits the ground, the impact causes his pistol to discharge.

All gang members of both sides flee the scene as the New York City Police respond to the gunshot. There is no time for the Dead Rabbits to retrieve Lance Gentles' prize spear that is lodged in the dead Limey's chest, along with the rabbit. Knowing where the fish net, spear and rabbit had to come from, the City Police take into custody, for questioning, many members of both the Irish and English gangs. However neither Lance Gentles nor anyone else is charged with any crime in the kill, because it is the creed of both gangs that:**"Nobody Knows Nothin"**.

Billy 'Lance Gentles' hurries off to join the U.S. Army, to some day again use his skill of taking down game with a home-made spear. The poor Irish youths of the city are many and they keep unified in their quest to uproot and pummel the older Limey youths, from New York City's Lower East Side. To plunge out the Limey gang from the Irish neighborhood, the Dead Rabbits lure them into city alleys to an awaiting ambush. The alleys run between high-rise buildings that have waiting female Irish gangsters on the rooftops. Once the Limeys are in range, the girls bombard them with city street bricks that they have stored away on the roofs. Kathy Shannahan and her Irish group drop down their nets to snag their victims so the Irish boys can batter them with clubs.

So that the Dead Rabbit thugs aren't injured by friendly fire raining down, they wear high top oversized derby hats stuffed with leather and rags. The derbies act as hard hats to protect their heads from the deluge of flying bricks. Those Irish warriors who sport these derby's that resemble New York City fireplugs, are called "THE PLUG UGLIES". Many Plug Uglies will be seen wearing these derbies in their city police mug shots.

To commemorate the success of the Dead Rabbit's initial confrontation with the Limeys, when Lance Gentles "knocked his man out", the Irish gang go into battle against their rivals carrying a battle flag—a rabbit impaled on a spear. This becomes the Irish gang's calling card—leaving a dead rabbit on any enemy's corpse. All Irish gang members who swear allegiance to the sect, rather they be man or woman, must obtain a lifetime tattoo of a rabbit impaled on a spear, to be worn on either upper arm. The Kelly clan members sport their rabbit tattoo on the left upper arm and put their tattoo of a double Kk on the upper right. Once the Irish gang successfully sweeps clean the Lower East Side of the Limeys and other gangs, they hang rabbits cadavers from city poles that line the boundaries of:**"The Tundra of Dead Rabbits"**.

Any rival gang member who makes the mistake of venturing into the Dead Rabbits' Den uninvited is found lying in an alleyway with a rabbit pelt around his neck that was used to strangle out the last breath. A few victims are found hanging in fish nets. However, so as not to deter visitors and tourists from coming into the Lower East Side of the city, to spend their earnings and enjoy the Irish Gangsters' new rackets of gambling, drinking and prostitution, billings are posted, of:

> **"All are welcome in on over,**
> **Spend money while you're at it,**
> **But if you've come to tread on us,**
> **You'll be dancin' with a Rabbit".**

For the next five years the Kelly clan of many does not get rich being Dead Rabbit Gangsters, but they do survive the tough times that the Irish endure during their early years in New York.

The young Irish grow older and whereas these Irish who were once raised entirely on the potato in their homeland of Ireland now enjoy the luxury of supplementing their spuds with choice steaks and lobster—all from the gang's crime booty. The all-Irish Dead Rabbits Gang is at the peak in 1860, New York City. The young teens that had formed the gang are now fully-grown men. The New York City Police who had gone from lackadaisically chasing small game hunters from city parks, to a relentless pursuit of the gang when the activity turned criminal, have well-stocked the city jails and the Tombs Prison with Irish hooligans, muggerines, thuganeers and arsonologists the likes of "Pyro Tommy" who get caught blowing up a police sub-station.

But the United States is on the fringe of a Civil War between the North and South, and the Northern Union Army is in dire need of recruits. The Union Army sends a representative to New York City's Tombs Prison, on direct orders from President Abraham Lincoln, to offer the outlaws and criminals an offer that is too good to refuse.

"Swearing an oath to the Union Army to fight the Rebels of the South and receive full pardons for your crimes, or rot out the Civil War in the Tombs."

The Irish criminals waste no time in getting in line to sign up.

With no physicals being required to join the Union Army, Irish female inmates cut their hair short and blend into the line with the boys. Girls that include Katherine "Snaggs" Shannahan use male first names to obtain their uniform and rifle.

"If the uniform fits and you can carry a carbine, you're in!"

This situation causes friction in the registration ranks, with the Irish stating that if they have to fight alongside those "damn Limeys", they would rather turn their weapons on the English than waste their ammo on the Rebels. Furthermore, there is no way an Irish Dead Rabbit going to take orders from an English Limey. So to counter this dilemma of mixing Irish New Yorkers with English New Yorkers, the Union Army creates an All-Irish Regiment: The New York Fighting 69th.

Now Kidd Kelly being the central figure in a Limey's murder investigation is given a special offer from the New York City Police: "Take a chance at going to trial for murder here in the Big City, being found guilty and hung in the Tombs, or become a spy for the Union Army with hopes that you won't be caught by the South and face a Rebel firing squad!" Kidd, without hesitation, accepts the latter choice saying, "Maybe the Rebel firing squad won't shoot straight." Kidd takes his Oath to the Union Army to spy for the Fighting 69th and vows not to desert his duty—for an Irishman lives or dies by his word.

The New York Fighting 69th are not the only Irish to take a vow to fight for their new country. The Irish immigrants who had come ashore to the New World at the southern port of New Orleans vow to fight for the Southern Cause. The Rebel South has also made an all-Irish Regiment of Louisiana. As the Luck of the Irish has it, these two Irish Regiments of opposite blue and gray colors meet on the battlefield in the early stages of the war.

Once the Louisiana Irish gray-bellies notice that the New York blue-bellies are flying the green flag of Erin County, Ireland, beside the Union Flag, the battle turns from a North against the South conflict, to a fight for the flag of the fatherland that reads:

"SONS OF ERIN, GO WHERE GLORY WAITS YOU."

The battle rages from sunup to sundown, with the Irish flag changing hands a half-dozen times. When the Irish soldiers from both sides run out of ammunition, they resort to "street fighting" with bayonets, clubs, knives, brass knuckles and lead-filled leather saps. It is only complete exhaustion on both sides that brings an end to the contest of juggling the Irish flag of Erin. The flag ends up in the hands of the New York 69th. Many Irishmen die at this battle and others waged in the years of the U.S. Civil War. When the war is finally over, those that survive return to their new homes in America, to take up where they left off.

Kidd Kelly had a successful campaign as a spy for the Union, sending many Southern spies to face a Northern firing squad. Kidd's intelligence work is brought to the attention of Union General Philip Sheridan.

After the war, Sheridan becomes the reconstructed U.S. Army's Commander of the West. Sheridan invites Kidd Kelly to go into the Western frontier with his Army and do intelligence reconnaissance for the U.S. Cavalry. Kidd is to travel through the Indian Territories disguised as a hardware trader in a covered wagon, to learn Indian strengths and movements. Kidd will be reporting to Lt. Colonel George Custer's 7[th]Cavalry on the Western plains. But first Kidd Kelly is given leave to return home to New York City and mull it over. On Kidd's return to the old neighborhood to visit his Kelly clan, he finds that the Irish Dead Rabbits Gang still controls the Lower East Side. However, a lot of his boyhood buddies are gone—some killed in the War and some killed by the Union Army, without getting into the Civil War.

During the peak of the War, the Union Army, running out of volunteers, drafted anyone of age who could not buy their way out with a 300 dollar donation to the Army's war chest. This was a condition that Union President Abraham Lincoln approved, and with the Irish population being poor, they could not put up the bounty to avoid the draft. Drafting the poor of New York City was considered unfair by the Irish, causing them to become riotous, some say with urging of southern infiltrators. The Union Army sent troops in to join the city police in fighting the rioters and before it was over, nearly two thousand people lost their lives—including Kidd's brother, the Catholic Priest Jack Kelly, Sr. along with the mother of Jack junior. Jack jr. was taken in by Auntie Kolleen Kelly. Families of those that were killed in the riots would later view John Wilkes Booth as a redeemer of vengeance, with talk that if Booth would have made his escape to New York City after he assassinated President Abraham Lincoln, "We'd a hid Booth out forever in the Lower East Side!"

With the return of Irish Civil War veterans to New York City, the city police department does not see their wish of the war fulfilled. Not all the city's Irish hooligans and thugaloons that were released from the Tombs Prison and jails to join the Union Army were disposed of in battle, nor did Kidd Kelly ever face that Rebel firing squad. With full pardons for their past crimes before the Civil War, the Irish veterans that do return alive are seasoned man-killers with a free paid education in gunology and explosives. The Dead Rabbits gangsters who have decided to return to New York City rather than to stay in the reconstructed U.S. Army return to their old ways of gang activity. However, these older Irishmen feel that the tag "Dead Rabbits" that the New York City Police put on their heads, is an outdated call for fully-grown men.

The Irish gangsters decide to call themselves the **"WHYOS"**, pronounced *Whaahoo*.

The name originates from the war-cry that the New York Fighting 69th shouted as they went into battle against the South in the Civil War. The war veterans now have a saying, "We were paid by the Union to kill, murder, ambush, snipe and cut the throats of sleeping Rebels. And being it's still war here on the streets of New York City against other gangs we can still do the same." Besides their usual gang activities of racketeering, gambling and houses of prostitution that they ran as Dead Rabbits, these more vicious WHYOS gangsters open up a fresh new endeavor. They rent themselves out as bodyguards and hit-men with a silent menu to customers for "puttin' in orders".

The hired killers of these WHYOS wear talons made of copper on their thumbs to pluck out the eyes of their victims, so as to bring them to their customers.

And with the Dead Rabbits, now WHYOS, slogan:

ONCE TATTOOED A MEMBER, THERE IS NOW NO WAY OUT OF THE GANG, SHORT OF DEATH.

Many Irish veterans of the Union Army decide to stay in the new reconstructed U.S. Army, rather than return to New York City gang life and live that slogan. In fact, so many that including girls still passing themselves off as "boys", one-third of the U.S. Army's 7th Cavalry will be made up of the Irish from New York.

Kidd Kelly's decision to go west is influenced by what General Philip Sheridan had told him prior to Kidd's return to New York. "Kidd, you can go back to the Big City, join your old gangster buddies, kill your enemy and hope the law don't hang you in the Tombs, or you can go west with my gang, kill your enemies, but with the knowledge that me, Phil Sheridan *is* the only law west of the Mississippi. With no civilian law enforcement agency of any type to get in the way."

WHYOS MENU

Give 'em a black eye		$ 3.00
	Two for	$ 5.00
Face broken up		$ 10.00
Jack 'em out with a blackjack		$ 10.00
Ear gnawed off		$ 15.00
	Two for	$ 25.00
Bust a limb, arm or leg		$ 15.00
	Two for	$ 25.00
Slice 'em up (knife job)		$ 25.00
	Two for	$ 40.00
Bringin' in the eye-balls (murder)		$100.00
		And up

CHAPTER FOUR
DEAD RABBITS WEST

The summer of 1867 sees Kidd Kelly doing U.S. Army Intelligence and Indian trading on the western plains of Kansas and Nebraska. On direct orders from General Phil Sheridan, Kidd is given a license to operate at will and a permit to eliminate anyone who halts his progress to obtain vital reconnaissance. No one can get in the way of the United States' expansion westward. To assist Kidd in his recon and dealing with the many uncivilized Indian Tribes he is to encounter, he is "issued" a young Miniconious Sioux Indian woman, about 18 years of age. The Army prefers an Indian woman over an Indian male to travel with Kidd, thinking that this orphaned girl will likely become attached to the handsome Kidd and stay loyal in her silence of his role and masquerade.

This young woman possesses strong Indian features of high cheek bones, a perfect set of white teeth, long black glossy hair and a pair of deep-set blazing dark eyes. She owns a fine-built muscled body, toned by hard labor at the orphanage ranch she was bought from. Because the orphanage had Indian children from many tribes, she is well versed in the many Indian languages and signs. She had become an orphan when a Kansas tornado swept down onto her tribe's Indian village at night. All, including her parents, were killed except for her. She was found in the only thing left standing in the field, a strong willow tree. Because of this, this orphaned Indian girl is called *Willowee,* "for one who does not break in the wind".

Due to the orphan ranch work, Willowee is good with horses and can ride or handle a team as good as any U.S. Cavalry pony soldier. Kidd instructs her in the use of weapons and Willowee becomes deadly accurate in the use of a hunting knife. Kidd gives her a large ivory-handled knife, the likes of a Jim Bowie. It is razor-sharp on the bottom edge from tip to guard. The top edge of the blade is honed sharp from tip back to crest. Willowee calls this gift from Kidd, "the knife that cuts both ways".

With this knife that cuts both ways, Willowee will save Kidd's hide from the fangs of a large striking rattlesnake by throwing the knife down the rattler's open throat, severing its head.

For the next several years, Kidd, with Willowee gather intelligence on the plains of Kansas and Nebraska by trading with the Indians out of their covered wagon. Kidd Kelly reports his recon to Lieutenant Colonel Custer's 7th Cavalry which is stationed at Fort Hays, Kansas. The fort sits along the Big Creek about one mile outside the town limits of Hays City, Kansas. But Kidd is not going directly to Fort Hays to report his observations because of the many Indians who linger about the fort. It is not to be known that Kidd is any way affiliated with the U.S. Army. Exchange of information will take place in the city limits of Hays. The saloons are the ideal locations for the soldiers to confer, for Indians are not allowed in establishments that serve alcohol. The two most frequented saloons of Hays City are Paddy Welch's Place and Tommy Drum's Saloon—both great Irish names. Lt. Colonel George Custer, being the commander of the 7th, not much of an alcohol consumer, and having his wife Elizabeth with him at Fort Hays, rarely attends the saloons of Hays City.

But George has a brother Thomas in the 7th Cavalry that is the opposite side of the coin. Unlike his brother George, Tom is not married and will never take that step. Although Fort Hays has an Officers Club that provides its own supply of alcohol, Captain Tom Custer does not mind doing his carousing with enlisted men and Cavalry scouts who do theirs in the saloons and dives of Hays City. Besides, Hays City is where the women are and many street fillies can be found at all hours to give soldiers company.

Kidd Kelly will do his recon reporting to Captain Tom Custer or another one of the 7th Cavalry who makes his second home Paddy Welch's Place. He is James "Dog" Kelley, a fellow Irishman and George Custer's orderly. The soldiers call him Dog because he is in charge of George Custer's attachment of the fine hunting hounds. George Custer could be seen quite often on the plains of Kansas with his greyhounds, running down antelope, deer, buffalo, bear, cougar or coyote. Whenever Kidd comes to Hays City to meet with soldiers, he never fails to bring Willowee. He has no intentions of leaving her alone at their various campsites to be carried off by hostile Indians or desperate white men. Kidd will rent a room at a local hotel and leave Willowee to do any needed shopping for provisions. But on occasion, Kidd will not hesitate in bringing Willowee along on his customary jaunts to join the boys of the 7th at Paddy Welch's or Tommy Drum's. Although Indians are not welcome in the saloons, no one dares to contest Willowee's presence. Her charm and grace are popular with the soldiers and if anyone were to attempt a fuss they would have to deal with the wrath of the 7th. Saloon owners also are too fond of the soldiers' business to deny one pretty little Indian girl.

During one of these times of the soldiers getting together for Indian business, cabareting, and carousing a group of Irish soldiers make a pact together. The initial force behind the creation of this Irish sect by several Kelly's of the 7th Cavalry who had been raised on the streets of New York City as Dead Rabbit Gang members, is the legend of two young Irish girls, 19 year-old Fanny Wiggins Kelly and her 5 year-old daughter Mary Kelly. Fanny Wiggins had married a Kansasourian Kelly, Josiah. Josiah Kelly had left New York to go west at the start of the Civil War. As he and his family traveled through the west with a small party, they were attacked by a band of Oglala Sioux Indians as they made camp 80 miles east of Fort Laramie, Wyoming. Josiah was out gathering firewood when three white men guarding the camp were killed by the Oglalas. Fanny Kelly and daughter Mary were carried off by the Indians. Many months later, Fanny was able to escape from her captors and tell of her ordeal. Fanny explains how the Oglalas' tattooed her and Mary above and below their lips to show ownership of white female slaves. White slaves were made to do the chores that Indian squaws thought degrading. Fanny was given a pony from an old Indian brave who attempted to win her over. The pony provided Fanny with a means of escape once she got the old man drunk on booze. However, little Mary Kelly was not so fortunate. Fanny tells of how an Indian teenage boy who was in charge of guarding Mary had molested and scalped her alive. The young buck then waved Mary's scalp in Fanny's face while bragging that it was his first scalping of a white. When Fanny's story reaches the Kellys of the 7th Cavalry, it so outrages them that they swear an oath to each other to avenge the senseless murder and mutilation of 5 year-old Mary Kelly.

The Irish Kelly clan has a motto:

> *"Wear the name,*
> *you're in the game,*
> *Kelly's the name, vengeance the game!"*

The Irish of Ole Ireland have another saying from the days of knights and chivalry:

"To tread on the smallest member of our clan will cause for the destruction of your greatest."

The Kelly's of the 7th Cavalry burn into their hearts the memory of little Mary and into their souls they forge the vow:

"Whosoever becomes the greatest of all Oglala Sioux will pay in blood for Mary's spilt blood."

Foregoes the beginning of the 7th Cavalry Irish Avengers who swear that Dead Rabbits curse:

"Death to those who tread on us!"

To seal their pact, the Kelly's and other Irish of the 7th Cavalry obtain lifetime tattoos of a human skull over crossed sabers with the number 7 jutting out of a jagged hole in the top of the skull. The skull and sabers are tattooed in black color. The number 7 is painted Irish green. The Irishmen wear their tattoo on the right forearm so to be viewed when in a handshake. The tattoo on some of the Irish joins the one of the New York City speared Dead Rabbit that lies on the left upper arm.

With one third of Custer's soldiers being of Irish descent, and most coming from the State of New York, the Dead Rabbits and Irish Avengers run rabid in the 7th Cavalry.

CHAPTER FIVE
IT'S A CIRCUS IN HAYS

In August, 1869, James Butler "Wild Bill" Hickok becomes the Sheriff of Ellis County, Kansas and the City Marshal of Hays City through the influence of his friends George Custer and George's wife Elizabeth "Libbie". Hickok was not elected but he took over the positions when the elected sheriff took leave. Hickok had fought for the North in the Civil War and was hired as a scout and courier for a short while by George, for the 7th Cavalry in 1867. Hickok did not stay long enough with the 7th for Kidd Kelly to make an acquaintance.

James Butler Hickok was not born William or Bill and a story is told among the soldiers on how Hickok became known as Wild Bill. It seems that when Hickok was a teenager, some bully tagged him "Duck Bill", for Hickok's long nose and protruding lips. Hickok could not whip the bully with his fists so he took up the art of handgunology. When Hickok achieved a "black (gun) belt" of the highest degree, he swore to himself that some day he would catch the arrogant bully and kill him. In the meantime, Hickok grew a large mustache to cover his dilemma. When Hickok finally crossed paths with the "author of Duck Bill", Hickok shut him up permanently. When asked why he killed him, Hickok said, "Because he called me Wild Bill." It was Hickok who altered the original dub to suit himself. But only a fool would now question Hickok to the original handle—for Wild Bill would soon be crowned "Prince of the Pistoleers".

Kidd thinks that Hickok and George Custer's friendship is one held together by an ego rivalry. Both were trying to outdo one another in their dress attire and both were keeping themselves lean, wearing long hair and trimmed facial hair. Each one was trying to outshine the other in their exploits so as to have their tales written up in eastern publications and dime novels. Both were always ready to pose for a camera. Kidd will observe George Custer and his wife "Libbie" on several occasions, come into Hays City to dine with Hickok and his female company. George would wear his parade best uniform and with gold braid, to impress the town citizens. Hickok would be attired in his best buckskin outfit with a silk sash about his waist. In his sash, Hickok would carry his two ivory-handled revolvers, tucked in, in cross-draw fashion, with an ivory-handled knife to match. George Custer would sport his gold decorated cavalry hat, while Hickok wore a large sombrero. But Libbie Custer would never fail to outshine these two flamboyant male showoffs, with her outfits of fine silk, satin and lace. Kidd will forever remember Libbie Custer as the most elegant white woman he ever lays eyes on. But, of course, to Kidd, no woman outshines his Willowee. Tom Custer will on occasion attempt to agitate his brother George and Hickok, by parading past their dinner table, wearing his two Medals of Honor, while George and Hickok engage in spinning some tale to some journalist.

This friendship that Marshal Hickok has with George and Libbie Custer, does not carry over to Tom Custer, Kidd, or any other soldier of the 7th Cavalry. When Hickok had become the lawman of Ellis County and Hays City, Kansas, he struck a deal with the officials that he would get paid a monthly salary, a certain amount per arrest and a percentage of any fine collected. Because of this "bounty" deal agreement, once Hickok took office as lawman, an increase in the number of Army soldiers that are arrested for disorderly or drunkenness take order. The soldiers get to thinking that whenever Hickok needs pocket money for his own drinking and gambling about the saloons of Hays City, he will just locate a drunken soldier who recently got paid. A soldier has a steady pay and there's no sense in arresting a broke drunk. Because of Hickok's practice of harassing the soldiers, he will have no other close friends of the 7th, besides George Custer and a Cavalry scout who goes by "California Joe".

California Joe is a mountain man. Rugged, bearded, smokes a tobacco pipe, smells like a bear and is described by George Custer as a half-man, half-horse, half-alligator. He's deadly with his knife or rifle and rides a mule named MAUD. Joe had been hired by George Custer to scout for the 7th Cavalry about the same time that Hickok had in 1867. The two struck up a friendship at that time. But when Hickok went on his way, Joe stayed on. The friendship, though, became airtight. Kidd would see the two of them, many times, drinking together in the saloons and dives of Hays City.

Kidd personally would not have an altercation with Hickok during Wild Bill's term as the lawman of Hays City and Ellis County, as did many soldiers of the 7th Cavalry. But Willowee has an incident with Marshal Hickok that Kidd thinks Wild Bill takes too seriously.

It happens in the Summer/Fall season of 1869 when a circus comes to Hays City. A woman by the name of Agnes Lake Thatcher owns a circus that Kidd thinks is more like a girlie show. Thatcher employs a group of scantily clad young women to ride horses bareback down the streets of Hays to promote the circus arrival. The attraction draws the attention of many city citizens, 7th Cavalry soldiers and most anyone in Hays those days. One of the circus acts is a shooting match where Thatcher challenges all comers against her employed marksman. When the match is over, Marshal Hickok takes advantage of the crowd at hand to put on an act of his own. Wild Bill does this act with his close friend California Joe. Hickok stands a wooden plank about the size of a man, six feet high and two feet wide, up against the wheel of a circus wagon. He paints an "X" with a piece of coal on the center of the plank. Hickok then walks off some good paces, about sixty feet, turns around and he, with California Joe face the plank while sucking on their tobacco pipes. Joe draws his long hunting knife as Hickok folds his own arms into his chest. Joe throws his knife at the plank while Wild Bill waits for the knife to leave Joe's hand. In a flash, Hickok draws his two ivory-handled Colts from his waistband and discharges both at the plank. A slug from each one of Hickok's revolvers beats Joe's knife to the plank putting two holes side by side, dead center in the "X". Joe's knife then follows the slugs directly into the holes. It is an act of marksmanship that Kidd has not seen done before.

This showmanship not only excites the crowd but greatly impresses the circus owner, Agnes Thatcher, and a young female circus performer named Molasses Mae. Mae is an olive skinned half Asian, half Black, whose act is tap dancing while whistling a tune. Mae invites Marshal Hickok to be her escort to the boxing match that the circus has scheduled for the evening. Wild Bill cannot refuse this beautiful girl's invitation. Agnes Thatcher has in her employment, a professional boxer who challenges all comers for prize money. The challenge is accepted by one of the 7th Cavalry Irishmen and an Avenger, Jerry Lanigan. Lanigan is a muscular pugilist of the Army and unbeaten at that.

The match looks to be a good one and everybody who is anybody about Hays City shows up for the fight. Many town citizens including the Mayor are in attendance. Marshal Hickok, with his young date, Molasses Mae, are alongside California Joe. This group is cheering for and has their money on Thatcher's pro boxer. Rooting for Lanigan are soldiers that include the brass of Fort Hays. Lt. Colonel George Custer is showcasing his Indian mistress, Monahseetah. George had told his wife Libbie that she could never go into Hays City after sundown due to the "rowdy element". Nighttime was saved for Monahseetah. George had selected the 22 year-old attractive

Indian from the Fort Hays "Squaw Corral". The 7th Cavalry had captured some 40 Indian females during the Washita Campaign. George had told his troopers, "I get the best, you all get the rest." George believed that Monahseetah had "fire" in her blood. Her Indian husband had showed up at the fort 6 months after her capture to lay claim to her. but Monahseetah refused to leave saying that she had a better life and she was now Custer's real wife. To convince her Indian ex-husband to leave her alone, she shot him in the kneecap, crippling him for life. Rumors lurked about Fort Hays that she bore George Custer a child and Libbie was quite curious about the yellow haired, fair skin baby boy on the fort grounds. But anyone who spoke of it at the fort was transferred out by the Lt. Colonel.

Alongside George and Monahseetah at this boxing match are Kidd Kelly and Willowee. Monahseetah cannot speak English so Willowee served as an interpreter for Custer. Monahseetah and Willowee became close friends with George commenting that they looked like the "Velvet Twins".

Now, Captain Tom Custer and soldier John Kelly, are flanked by their Army issued squaws at the fight. Jim "Dog" Kelley is accompanied by one of Custer's hounds to "howl for the 7th's honor". All 7th Cavalry money is riding on the pugilest, Jerry Lanigan.

The boxing match starts out to be a close encounter for several rounds, before Lanigan starts to toy with the prize-fighter. As Lanigan dances around his opponent, he looks out into the audience to make glances and gestures toward Hickok's date, Molasses Mae. Mae seems pleased, but Lanigan's antics are aggravating Marshal Hickok so that the marshal begins to twist the ends of his mustache with the fingers of one hand. This is a habit of Hickok's that Kidd Kelly has seen him do on an occasion when a civilian had threatened to kill Hickok. On that occasion, Hickok had fingered his mustache with one hand the instant before he pulled one of his revolvers with the other hand and shot the man dead. Lanigan plays with the pro boxer for a couple more rounds and then puts him down for good in the 7th. It is the 7th round for the 7th Cavalry. The soldiers are jubilant as they collect their winnings from the Hays City citizens who had bet on the circus boxer. Lanigan picks up his prize money and then waves it at Mae, who is still in Hickok's company. She accepts Lanigan's offer to join him in spending it, which again infuriates Hickok. A dangerous situation for Lanigan, but there are too many soldiers about so Hickok has no choice but to accept the embarrassment of Lanigan walking off with his date. It would be an embarrassment that Hickok would not forget. Lanigan, with

Mae now in hand and the boys of the 7th in pursuit, marches over to Paddy Welch's Place to celebrate the victory. Female circus performers follow suit.

With the circus now over for the evening, Kidd walks Willowee back to their hotel room, where he tells her to settle in for the night. Kidd returns to Paddy Welch's to rejoin the Lanigan victory celebrations. It irritates Willowee that Kidd is leaving her alone this night. So she begins to drink from a bottle of wine she has in the room. After the first glass of wine is downed, she begins to tremor with thoughts of lily-white-skinned, scantily-clad female circus performers, pawing over her handsome Kidd at Paddy Welch's. After the second glass of wine, Willowee's tremors start to rattle the furniture in the room. On the third glass, Willowee goes volcanic. She blasts out of the hotel room to fly down to where the circus wagons are parked. With all of Thatcher's performers about the various restaurants, saloons and dives, there is no one at the wagons to stop her action. Willowee helps herself to one of the scanty outfits that barely covers her breasts. She mounts a circus horse with intentions of putting on a variety act of her own. She gallops down the streets of Hays while standing on the bareback horse. Holding the reins of the horse with one hand, Willowee fires a pistol several times into the air with the other. As she rides past Paddy Welch's, there are already several soldiers and circus people out front on the boardwalk. Willowee puts away the pistol into one of her boots and draws out that ivory-handled knife that "cuts both ways". While riding the horse in circles in front of the saloon, she throws the knife and torpedoes the Paddy Welch sign that swings in the wind. She redraws the pistol to continue her circling and shooting.

The 7th Cavalry soldiers hoot and holler urging Willowee on as Monahseetah wardances on the Paddy Welch boardwalk. But then Marshal Hickok rides up on the scene and he thinks it no laughing matter. He rides his horse alongside Willowee's to take hold of her horse's reins. Hickok yanks the reins causing the circus horse to stumble and throw Willowee into a large puddle of mud that lies in front of a water trough. Willowee gets to her feet unhurt but totally covered in mud. She can only laugh as the soldiers whistle and cat call at the Indian girl who fills out the scanty outfit more strikingly than any circus girl. Kidd Kelly thinks it as some of the most excitement that Hays City has witnessed in some time. But Marshal Hickok sees it differently. Wild Bill attempts to arrest Willowee for firing a weapon in the city limits and possible horse stealing. His actions are about to start a riot by the soldiers, when circus owner Thatcher comes on the scene. Thatcher refuses any horse thief charge and jokingly comments that Willowee should join her show. Kidd asserts himself into the controversy and demands to pay Willowee's fine for disorderly on the spot. Marshal Hickok, anxious to get his portion of another city fine into his pocket, gets his satisfaction.

Agnes Thatcher invites the marshal to join her and some friends for dinner. Wild Bill offers his arm to his future wife. As Hickok and Thatcher stroll down the boardwalk and out of sight, Kidd comments to the Paddy Welch crowd, "She sure don't look near Mae, but then Mae don't have a fat purse near the likes of a circus owner." Kidd wipes the mud off Willowee, gives her a shirt, and the two proceed into Paddy Welch's to join the cabaret.

Captain Tom Custer has an incident of his own with Marshal Wild Bill Hickok, that Kidd Kelly thinks hilarious. But again, not the Marshal. Tom Custer is a fine soldier as can be attested by his two Medals of Honor. Tom is also an expert billiard pool player of which he is equally proud. Tom could not, or would not, turn down a pool playing challenge if it came his way. He was hard to beat when on his game, but if he were to be beaten, he was a good sport at losing, if he thought it a fair game.

One night Tom gets into a pool tournament in Hays City with some town citizens. He beats all comers until he is down to the last man who has beat all at his table.The two play at the other man's table where Tom loses two out of three and the championship. Tom Custer explodes at the final results, blaming the faulty unbalanced pool table. Tom requests a replay at the pool table he was winning at.However, the bartender, having the final say, refuses. Being a man of his word, Tom Custer pays off the victor then storms out of the front doors of the pool hall. Within minutes, back through the front door, returns Tom Custer—this time riding his horse. Tom urges the horse up onto the faulty pool table to allow the four-legged beast to trample out a 7th Cavalry dance. However, the jittery animal releases his bowels, causing all saloon pool hall clientele to scatter for drier ground. Captain Tom Custer spurs his horse off the manure engulfed sport apparatus, while laughing like a hyena, at his excitement of realizing that he has successfully renovated the billiard table into a craps table. Tom rides out the front door to be greeted by Marshal Wild Bill Hickok and his troop of drinking buddies. Tom is outnumbered and does not have the cavalry support that Willowee had had with her incident with the Marshal. Tom Custer is arrested for disorderly by Hickok and the horse is citied for "discharging a weapon in public". With no money on hand on account of losing his in the pool tournament, Tom and his horse spend the night incarcerated in Hays City. Brother George Custer arrives in the morning to pay Tom's fines and to fatten Marshal Hickok's small change purse. Marshal Hickok's practice of arresting many soldiers of the 7th Cavalry for minor infractions does not sit too well with the boys. It seems to them that the harassment increased after the Jerry Lanigan – Mae incident. It gets to the point that many soldiers of the 7th mutter that if they ever catch Wild Bill Hickok without his tin star, they'll whip the "sheep dip out of his hide".

But it seems that the good citizens of Hays City and Ellis County also get fed up with Hickok's ways about Hays, in the short time he's the law. In the election for sheriff November 1869, the citizens vote in Hickok's Deputy, Peter Lanihan over Wild Bill. After being the sheriff and marshal for just 5 months, Hickok leaves office and Hays City, on New Year's Day, January 1, 1870. Wild Bill Hickok is out of Ellis County without his tin star before any 7th Cavalry soldiers can make good their vow to whip him proper. But Hickok did manage to kill 2 civilians in the short time he was the Marshal of Hays. A Bill Mulvey on Front Street and a Sam Strawhun during a disturbance in the Leavenworth Beer Saloon.

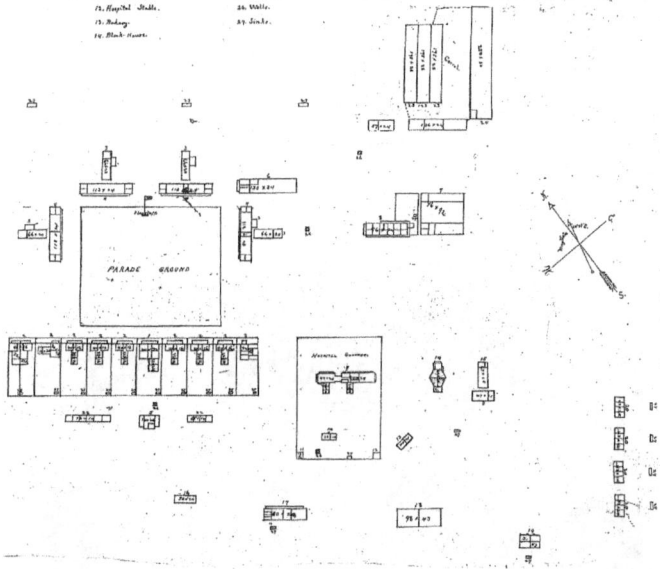

7th Soldiers Tents Fort Hays

7th Cavalry Officers Barracks

Courtesy Kansas State Historical Society

Left to right: Wesley Merritt, David McM.Gregg, Sheridan,
Henry E. Davis (standing), James H. Wilson and Alfred Torbert.

General Phil Sheridan,
The Only God West Of The Mississippi

George Armstrong Custer When A General

Courtesy of Kansas State Historical Society

"Libbie" And George Custer

Custer with his dogs

Courtesy Of Kansas State Historical Society

GENERAL AND MRS. CUSTER dine in front of their tents on the banks of Big Creek near New Fort Hays during the summer of 1869. A dog sits alongside Custer, and an orderly stands in waiting. (Photo from Kansas State Historical Society.)

THIS WOODEN STOCKADE at New Fort Hays served to corral the more than 50 Indian women and children captured by Custer at the Battle of the Washita. Mo-nah-see-tah and three braves that Custer took hostage were also held there. Two of these braves and a squaw were killed there when the Indians attacked the guards while being moved from the stockade to the guardhouse, the building with three narrow horizontal windows. The corral was 15 feet high and had a walkway around it for the guards. (Photo from Kansas State Historical Society.)

Courtesy Of Kansas State Historical Society

CHEYENNE WOMEN AND CHILDREN captured at the Battle of the Washita were photographed by William S. Soule at Ft. Dodge, while on their way to the stockade at Ft. Hays. This is only part of the 55 or more persons captured; at least another 10 persons were in the group. Judging from his right hand, which appears to have the fourth finger mangled, the man at the left is John O. Austin, chief of scouts at Ft. Dodge and later interpreter a Camp Supply.

Women Of Fort Hays Squaw Corral

Courtesy Of Kansas State Historical Society

James Butler "Wild Bill" Hickok

Moses Milner, California Joe
Courtesy Of Kansas State Historical Society

CHAPTER SIX
SHOOT THE HOUND

K idd Kelly remembers it as a hot summer day of July 1870, when he and Willowee are camped along the Big Creek, just outside of Fort Hays, Kansas. During breakfast Kidd mentions to Willowee to load the wagon. They will be going into Hays City before nightfall, where he intends to rent a room with hot bath for several days. The muddy Big Creek just ain't getting the job done. It's early evening by the time they get started on their journey into Hays. Willowee comments to Kidd that she does not like the looks of this day's sunset, with thunder clouds rolling along the horizon.

"Looks like evil on the prowl for its victim this night."

Kidd dismisses her statement and uneasiness as just some more of her Indian superstition. But little does he realize at this time, that it will turn out to be no jabberwocky.

Once in Hays, Kidd rents a room where he and Willowee clean up for an evening on the town. They have dinner at the hotel steakhouse and then begin their waltz on over to Paddy Welch's Place to join some 7th Cavalry soldiers who should be there celebrating a birthday. Because of Willowee's uneasiness this night, brought on by her vision of the sunset, she urges Kidd not to go about the city unarmed—a practice Kidd always follows—but he assures her that he will, to settle her down.

"There'll be no trouble tonight, my little red darlin'," Kidd says. "We'll be among friends."

Kidd snickers to himself as he observes his little "red darling" hone her knife that cuts both ways, before she slips it in her moccasin boot. On their arrival at Paddy Welch's, the two are greeted by several of the Irish soldiers, who, with female companionship, are already having a celebration. The group is all gathered about the saloon piano player, while belching out Irish songs. Kidd recognizes the Irish crooners as Sergeant John Ryan and soldiers Jerry Lanigan, John Kelly and Jim "Dog" Kelley. Dog Kelley is playing his harmonica while one of the hound dogs, who he has given beer to, howls along. The girls in the bunch are Hays City residents, with the one alongside Jerry Lanigan being Molasses Mae.

Mae had quit the circus life for a barmaid role in Paddy Welch's. Kidd and Willowee join in for some drinking, singing and dancing the Irish Jig. The Jig is a dance that Willowee takes to quite easily, saying it's just a stepped-up version of an Indian dance that she had learned as a child. When not doing the Jig, Willowee joins the piano player and Dog Kelley with his harmonica, in blasting out Irish tunes on her wooden Indian flute. After an hour or so into the merry making, John Kelly and Jerry Lanigan comment that they are going over to Tommy Drum's Saloon with their female company to continue their carousing. Kidd and Willowee decide to join in. Dog Kelley, with his faithful hound at his feet, tags along.

Sgt. Ryan chooses to keep with the action at Paddy Welch's. When the squad of Irish soldiers, their female dates, and the hound, arrive at Tommy Drum's this thundering, lightening evening, they go to a table at the rear of the saloon. Kidd steps to the bar to order a bottle of whiskey, champagne for the girls and beef jerky for the hound. While standing at the bar, Kidd detects the aroma of cherry tainted tobacco smoke. It's the kind that Wild Bill Hickok and California Joe are known to smoke in their pipes. Kidd looks toward the group of men that are drinking at the bar to notice that it is Hickok and Joe with another fellow unknown to Kidd. California Joe is still a scout for George Custer's 7th Cavalry, so Hickok must be in town on a visit to his 'ole buddy Joe'. Kidd gives the group no attention as he gathers up his bar order and moves on over to his party's table. After just one drink, soldiers Lanigan and John Kelly become irritated that Hickok is in the saloon, drinking and being clamorous with his two buddies—a situation that Hickok used to harass soldiers for doing when he was the town marshal. Lanigan and John Kelly decide to go to the bar and voice their opinions.

Hickok is not displaying his two ivory-handled Colt pistols that he usually wears. Current County Sheriff Lanihan has a rule that guns are not to be worn in town. However, this rule does not keep some from packing hidden ones, as Kidd was doing. As far as Kidd knows, Lanigan and John Kelly are not armed. As the two soldiers approach the bar, Lanigan stands next to Hickok, who pays no attention to the two soldiers. Lanigan stares into the wall mirror behind the bar and at Hickok's reflection. Knowing that Hickok once had the eye for the ex-circus girl Mae, Lanigan starts in. "Ya, Mae is the best little filly I've ever rode, Wild Bill. Too bad you never got the chance to try some a that sweet molasses."

Hickok doesn't flinch as he keeps to his own conversation with California Joe and the other man.

"I'm talkin' to you, Hickok!" Lanigan barks as he grabs Wild Bill by the arm, to spin him around and knock Hickok to the floor.

John Kelly, standing by, comments to California Joe to stand aside. "It's a fair fight that Hickok's got a comin'."

But Kidd Kelly knows it won't be a fair fist fight because no one holds a chance against the pugilist, Jerry Lanigan. Lanigan knocks Hickok down a second time when Wild Bill tries to get on his feet.Lanigan makes a statement that causes Kidd to rise from his own chair, "I'm gonna whip the duck dung outa ya, Duck Bill." Calling Hickok "Duck Bill" is a mistake that had already cost one man his life.

Kidd starts to walk to the one-sided scuffle before it gets out of hand, as Lanigan and John Kelly laugh aloud at Hickok's dilemma. But before Kidd can get there, the two soldiers' jeering is cut short by the cracking sound of four quick gunshots. Hickok, while still lying on the floor, had swiftly drawn two two-shot derringer pistols from his boots, one a boot, and fired the lead contents in the direction of the cackling soldiers. Lanigan and John Kelly had brung their fists to a gun fight. And there's no man alive whose fist can provide the knock-down punch delivered by a .41 caliber Williamson Derringer. Hickok's shots found their mark, dropping the two soldiers to the same floor that Wild Bill had occupied. Kidd Kelly draws for his hidden revolver to retaliate for the two shot soldiers. But before Kidd can accomplish his move, California Joe and the other man with Hickok, had already drawn their hidden weapons with dead aim on Kidd and Jim "Dog" Kelley. Kidd, though knowing that Joe still scouts for the 7th Cavalry, now sees that Joe's loyalty lies with his pal Wild Bill. Kidd and Dog Kelley are useless in the situation and must drop their weapons. But California Joe is not as trigger happy as Hickok, so he suggests to Wild Bill that it would be wise for them to depart while they hold the upper hand.

Before Hickok's party can leave Drum's Saloon, Kidd looks Wild Bill in the eye and spits out a vow, "Hickok, you are mighty tough when your back is so well covered by other guns, but the day will come when your back will not be so well protected. And when that day does come, I'LL BE THERE!"

Willowee, hearing her partner Kidd's remark to Hickok, and recalling her vision of sunset, darts to wedge herself between Kidd and Hickok, while drawing her Bowie. Kidd, acting instinctively, pushes her aside. Kidd believes that Hickok may wish to shoot him for the remark, but he knows that Wild Bill has spent the ammo of the two Derringers on the two downed soldiers. California Joe pulls Hickok by the arm and out the front door of the saloon in hopes of ending the whole matter, and to join the third man at the railed horses. But the *whole* matter is not yet over. Jim Kelley's hound breaks loose from Mae, who had been restraining the dog by its collar. Being a man's best friend, who, unlike California Joe, is loyal to the boys in blue, the dog dashes for his prey and takes hold of Hickok's leg.

Wild Bill, now next to his horse, pulls the rifle from the saddle holster and drives the butt of the weapon into the hound's skull. Hickok twirls his rifle and fires, blasting out the brains of Dog Kelley's prize musical four-legged hunting buddy. Kidd has to restrain Jim Kelley from making a fatal lunge for the re-armed Hickok. Hickok, Joe and the unknown third man mount their horses and turn to ride out of town in the darkness of night. The third man of Hickok's group is heard to holler, "Ya, blue bellies should-in-na messed with the Prince a the Pistoleers!" It is a squeaky southern accent voice that Kidd Kelly will never forget.

As lightening bolts light up the sky, Kidd stands in the street in front of Tommy Drum's to watch Hickok and his two cohorts depart Hays City. He raises his fist and snorts aloud, "You all can run but you can't hide, 'cause Hell's behind ya!"

Sgt. Ryan and several other soldiers arrive on the scene from Paddy Welch's, along with the County Sheriff Peter Lanihan. All drawn by Hickok's rifle shot to the hound. Everyone now tends to the wounded soldiers in the saloon, that Willowee and Molasses Mae are attempting to help to their feet. Soldier Jerry Lanigan is slightly wounded and able to get up. John Kelly, however, is much worse off and unable to stand on his own.Kidd looks John Kelly (who had been shot in the back and is losing consciousness) in the eyes and swears his third vow this night, "No matter how long it takes us, John, we WILL GET HICKOK!"

But it's a promise to a dying soldier and Irishman.

Sheriff Lanihan volunteers a wagon to transport the two wounded soldiers to the Fort Hays Army hospital. Kidd thanks the lawman, but tells him not to concern himself with going after Wild Bill Hickok. For this is a

U.S. Army situation and, "The 7th Cavalry will take care of its own." Sgt. Ryan takes John Kelly and Jerry Lanigan to the fort by wagon, where he recruits other soldiers to return to Hays City and begin a hunt for Hickok. However, by the time Sgt. Ryan returns to Hays City with some troopers, Hickok's trail has gone cold. Soldier John Kelly dies from his bullet wound but Jerry Lanigan will shortly recover from his.

When the killing of John Kelly by Wild Bill Hickok is reported to General Phil Sheridan, "The only god west of the Mississippi" lays down his commandment:

"One cannot sin against Sheridan's Army and go unpunished."

For a civilian to kill a U.S.Army soldier that has been awarded the Congressional Medal of Honor, is a mortal sin! (John Kelly had earned his for bravery and gallant conduct at Dog Creek, Nebraska, on July 8, 1869.) Sheridan demands that Wild Bill Hickok, the back shooter, be brought in "Dead or Alive". It won't be any easy task to fulfill, and the Kelly's of the 7th Cavalry have no idea when or if they will be able to get Hickok.

Because California Joe had sided with Wild Bill Hickok and assisted in his escape, a dangerous toxic atmosphere will lurk about Fort Hays for Joe. Although Joe had not shot either of the Irish soldiers, most think Joe a turncoat. George Custer warns his scout Joe that he cannot protect him from the perilous rudiments that linger about the fort. "Joe," George suggests, "It would be good sense for you to get as much space possible between yourself and those that wear the skull and sabers. The fuse to your execution is about to be lit, and word is, Joe, that the rabid Irishmen intend to make your mule Maud, the dinner after meal. Not even I, George Custer, the greatest General of the Civil War, can tame a Dead Rabbit."

California Joe wisely takes Custer's advice and Joe rides his mule Maud out of Fort Hays into the darkness of night. Joe's career as an Army scout for the 7th Cavalry comes to an end. But Joe's career is not the only one that changes direction shortly after the Hays City confrontation. 7th Cavalry soldier, Jerry Lanigan, becomes hypnotic to the ex-circus girl turned barmaid, Molasses Mae's charms, transforming him into a SLACKER. Lanigan deserts from the 7th Cavalry and breaks his pact as an Irish Avenger, to run off with his new found love. The pact that the Irish Avengers have made to each other is a deadly pact—one that once made cannot be broken. Just as the tattoo of skull and sabers is for life, so stands the vow to avenge any member who has been treaded upon. And the Kelly's of the 7th think

Lanigan owes it the most, to avenge John Kelly. For it was he who started the confrontation with Wild Bill Hickok that led to John Kelly's death. The Irish Avengers of the 7th Cavalry will not forgive or forget Lanigan for his desertion and reneging.

As Kidd Kelly puts it to the Union Army, while living on the streets of New York City.

"An Irishman lives or dies by his word."

Tommy Drum's Saloon

Courtesy Of Kansas State Historical Society

CHAPTER SEVEN
HE AIN'T NO SCHOOL KID

In the spring of the year 1871, George Custer receives orders to move his 7th Cavalry to the state of Kentucky, to confront the growing problem of civilian whiskey bootleggers and the all-white-man Ku Klux clan. George does not approve of harassing American citizens when there are plenty of Indian savages on the western plains, to run down but it is a federal problem and the government has no civilian federal law enforcement agency to handle the situation. A skeleton crew of the 7th Cavalry maintains Fort Hays and Kidd Kelly and his companion Willowee continue their recon on the western plains.

Jim "Dog" Kelley is thinking of retirement from his U.S. Army life and takes leave to scout out a civilian way of life. The Ole Dog is wanting to locate a western boom town so as to go into the hunting dog breeding business. Buying into a saloon or restaurant establishment is also on Kelley's agenda. Jim Kelley makes a trip to the growing town of Abilene, Kansas, to look into its potential. He travels alone, sans his U.S. Army uniform, but as usual, Kelley takes along for company, one of the 7th's hound dogs. Once in Abilene, Jim and his mutt stop at a saloon that has out front an unusual sign, of a bull animal with large reproductive organs. The saloon is named the BULLS HEADS TAVERN. Inside the tavern are only the bartender and a baby-faced young man drinking at the bar. Dog Kelley steps up to the bar, near the young man, to order two beers to quench the thirsts of himself and his hound. The bartender serves up two beers along with an offer to purchase Kelley's good-looking hound dog. Jim Kelley declines the offer, but informs the bartender that there may be some good hunting dogs available in the near future. Kelley orders a shot of whiskey, which once downed gives Jim the gall to wisecrack to the young man who has so far been silent, "What, no school today, kid?"

The bartender quickly cuts in, to prevent Dog Kelley from saying another word. "Keep me in mind, fella," the bartender says. "I'll need a fast hound to chase antelope. You can find me here, I own this here tavern," he continues as he puts his hand out in introduction. "My name is Ben Thompson, and this here kid is John Wesley Hardin. He's a Texan who has killed more damn Yankee soldiers in Texas after the Civil War than I did fighting 'em in it."

Jim "Dog" Kelley swallows his chewing tobacco as he nervously puts out his hand to shake Thompson's. Kelley, having read dime novels, is well aware of the two men that occupy this Bulls Head Tavern and their gun-fighting reputations. Kelley breaks into a sweat as he looks at Hardin's cold stare, reflecting in the mirror behind the bar. "I apologize for my bad joke, Mr. Hardin." Kelley stutters at the mirror.

"I've killed men for cracks like that," the kid Hardin finally speaks as he bends down to pet Kelley's hound. "I'm drinkin' rye," Hardin hints.

"Bottle of your best rye whiskey, Ben," Kelley quickly counters. "If you like the hound, Mr. Hardin, he's yours," Kelley adds, hoping it will be a fair exchange for his own life.

The two southern boys, Hardin and Thompson, now detecting Kelley's uneasiness, start to laugh. "No offense, old timer," Hardin remarks. "Join me in drinkin' the rye and no need to call me mister. I like to go by Wesley."

Jim "Dog" Kelley relaxes for the first time being and feels safe in introducing himself as a soldier of Custer's 7th Cavalry.

"I come from the South myself, boys," Kelley starts. "Custer talked me into joining up, just to handle his fine bunch of huntin' hounds. The boys of the 7th call me Hound Dog. I'm now lookin' for a town to start a dog-breedin' business."

"Hound Dog" Kelley has the Luck of the Irish this day, in crossing paths with these two Texans who have an appreciation for fine huntin' dogs and those who care for them. A friendship seems to be made as Kelley inquires about the town of Abilene and its citizens. He receives a surprise when Thompson jaws about the new Abilene town marshal.

"That Marshal Hickok is givin' me hell over my tavern sign out front," Ben says, referring to the bull sex organs on display. "Says it's indecent."

"Wild Bill Hickok?" Dog Kelley cuts in.

"Yea," Ben answers. "Damn Yankee needs a killin'."

Kelley now tells Thompson and Hardin the story of the Hays City confrontation between Hickok and the Irishmen of the 7th Cavalry, including the part where Wild Bill killed one of George Custer's prize hounds. As Kelley ends his tale, the sound of horses are heard coming to a halt out front of the Bulls Head. In through the front door struts a striking looking woman, followed by a man. The man sits at the table near the front door, to gaze out the window. The female approaches the bar while tap dancing and whistling. Dog Kelley immediately recognizes the antics of the olive skinned girl. It is Molasses Mae, the ex-circus performer who had run off with the 7th Cavalry deserter, Jerry Lanigan. Kelley now takes a good gander at the man sitting at the table. It is Jerry Lanigan. Kelley excuses himself from his two new Texas friends to approach the slacker's table. Jerry Lanigan does not recognize the out-of-uniform Kelley until the Dog stands before him.

"Lanigan," Kelley asserts. "You took an oath to the 7th Cavalry. But over that, you carry the mark and wear the name of an Irish Avenger. And if you wear the name, you can't forsake the game. You're a rogue, Lanigan, and you're goin' back to Fort Hays on or over your saddle."

"I'll be takin' no more orders from the likes of you Kelly's,"Lanigan answers as he rises from his chair while reaching for his revolver.

But Jim "Dog" Kelley has already drawn his and fires twice. Lanigan, who is quicker with his fists than he is on the draw for his pistol, drops to the floor of the Bulls Head, fatally shot. The ex-honorable pugilist of the 7th Cavalry dies a dishonorable soldier, Irish Avenger and Traitor. Dog Kelley walks back to the bar to have another whiskey as he holsters his pistol.

John Wesley Hardin speaks, "Kelley. You beat your ex-buddy there, but I saw your pistol come out of your holster. Word is that Hickok's so fast that the human eye can't see him pull his. I suggest you leave without delay. You're a long piece from your 7th Cavalry, and as sure as I'm a Texan, Hickok's gonna be a comin'."

"Appreciate the advice, Wesley," Dog Kelley replies. "But an Irishman never leaves an unfinished bottle of good whiskey. And we ain't finished this here one yet."

Mae, who has stood motionless and silent at the bar while things transpired, now comments, "Well, looks like my ride ends here. Could this place use a little Molasses?"

"Sure, girl," Ben answers. "You look like you could sweeten up the place. A room goes with the job."

Before Dog Kelley and Wesley Hardin can finish that good bottle of rye whiskey, through the front doors of the Bulls Head Tavern, barges new town Marshal Wild Bill Hickok accompanied by his shadow, California Joe and his trusty rifle.

Hickok notices the dead man lying on the floor and demands, "Who's the killer?"

Before Dog Kelley can say a word, John Wesley Hardin steps away from the bar, pushing Kelley aside. The young Hardin stands tall, displaying two revolvers tucked in his belt, cross draw, to match Hickok's style. Hardin speaks while looking Hickok in the eye. "Well, if it ain't Wild Bill Hickok. I'm John Wesley Hardin. Did ya come to shoot the hound, Wild Bill?" Hardin pricks, referring to Kelley's story of Hickok killing the 7th Cavalry's dog in Hays City.

Ben Thompson, still behind the bar, reaches under it and lays a sawed-off shotgun down on top of the bar. "No damn Yankee's arrestin' nobody in my house!" Ben demands.

Hickok and California Joe, who, like Dog Kelley also read the dime novels, are well aware of the two Texas gunmen that stand before them. But Dog Kelley knows that Hickok and Joe are two of equal reputations that include not backing down to anyone. Kelley can feel the tension in the tavern as he thinks to himself that he could be bearing witness to one helluva handgun battle. But before any of these four man-killers touch their weapons, Hickok recalls the flashy looking Molasses Mae, who for the second time is frozen in her tracks against the wall. Wild Bill now takes a second and closer look at the dead man on the floor, to recognize him as Jerry Lanigan, the 7th Cavalry soldier who had started the confrontation in Hays City.

"Well, I'll be damned," Marshal Hickok remarks. "This man needed killin'. I'm beholden to the gentleman who spared me the task."

Hickok looks back at Mae and states a wise crack that is intended to prod her for leaving him and walking off with Lanigan that day in Hays City when Thatcher's Circus paid a visit. "Life's tough, Mae, when you're a Loser Chooser."

California Joe, who has now recognized the un-uniformed Jim Kelley from his own days scouting for the 7th Cavalry, taps Marshal Hickok on the shoulder, while commenting, "No call us being here, Marshal. The Army can pick up their own trash."

Hickok and Joe slowly and cautiously back out the front doors of the Bulls Head, to end the stand off.

"Hickok's the one who needs a killin'." Thompson remarks for a second time once Wild Bill and Joe are out of earshot.

"You'll have to kill 'im yourself, Ben, if you're a wanting it done," the young Wesley answers. "I hear he's as quick and deadly as me. Any gun play 'tween us be a tie. And just like runnin' your horse to beat a smokin' loco train to the crossin', TIES LOSE!"

Dog Kelley thanks his two Texas friends for their backup, and as a show of gratitude, again he offers his fine female hunting hound with the explanation that Mr. Custer has plenty. Hardin refuses the offer but Thompson gladly accepts the 7th Cav's hound.

Thompson and Hardin assist Kelley in picking up Lanigan's body and putting it over his horse. Kelley's last words as he mounts his own horse to ride are "Don't get too close to the marshal boys cause some blood thirsty rabid Irishmen will be paying this town of Abilene a visit." On his ride back to Fort Hays, Dog Kelley, not wanting to soil the military cemetery with the corpse of a deserter, buries Lanigan on the lonely prairie of Kansas.

In the years to come, Jim "Dog" Kelley's inclination that he almost bore witness to a major handgun duel, will prove out. For Wild Bill will never lose a pistol duel and is so quick and accurate that his opponents, when facing him hardly ever get a shot off. With his marksmanship, Hickok earns the knighthood, "Prince of the Pistoleers". Hickok's teammate, California Joe, is described by U.S. Army soldiers as a full-hair-headed red-whiskered accurate and deadly rifleman killer.

Now, on the other side of that potential battle line that crossed the Bulls Head Tavern of Abilene, Kansas, was John Wesley Hardin. Although he was only nineteen years of age when facing Hickok, he had already been killing in his home state of Texas, since he was sixteen. Hardin later claims to have killed some 40 men and will be called the most feared man in Texas and the "fastest gun alive". Now Hardin's sidekick that day in the Bulls Head was Ben Thompson. He will achieve his own kill count of some 30 victims. He is the gunman who actually shot the pistol out of a foe's hand, in a gunfight at a saloon in Ogalala, Nebraska. Bat Masterson will tag Ben Thompson, "The West's most deadly gunman".

These four gunmen who faced off in the Bulls Head Tavern in the year 1871 are so deadly and dauntless that, to a man, they will only be done in by ambush and backshooters. Yes, a gun duel 'tween these two tandems of gunologist WOULD HAVE set the standards for a PhD in handgunology.

Kidd Kelly learns from Jim "Dog" Kelley that Wild Bill Hickok is the town Marshal of Abilene, but he must wait until the fall of the year to take leave of his duties. Kidd recruits five other Irish Avengers from Fort Hays and along with Dog Kelley, it's seven Avengers for the 7th Cav's honor. However, it's not to look as if it's a U.S. Army operation, so the seven Avengers ride for Abilene out of uniform. By the time these seven Irishmen arrive in Abilene, they discover Wild Bill Hickok is keeping pace with his growing reputation of not lasting long at anything he does in life. The un-uniformed soldiers visit the Bulls Head Tavern, where Dog Kelley and the other six are immediately recognized by Ben Thompson as the bloody boys of the 7th that Kelley foretold would pay Abilene a visit. After introductions, Ben tells the Irishmen that Hickok had been relieved of his lawman position by Abilene vigilantes. Marshal Hickok had had an altercation with Thompson's friend Phil Coe that lead to Wild Bill and California Joe being run out by the Abilene mob.

"He shot down my friend Coe for no call!" are the Texan's words as he relates the story of what occurred.

Phil Coe, who had been running Ben's gambling and prostitution operations at the Bulls Head, was using Molasses Mae in the role of a street filly.

Marshal Hickok demanded a piece of the action on the streets of "his town". Coe refused Hickok's extortion demands, so Wild Bill looked for an opportunity to "gun 'im". Ben Thompson also thought that Hickok had desires for Mae, and was jealous of Coe for it. Hickok found his chance to get Coe one day, when drinking in the Alamo Saloon across from the Bulls Head. Coe was in the Bulls Head when he noticed some stray dog outside on the street trying to mount the female hunting hound that Jim Kelley had given to Ben Thompson. It was a stray dog of low character, not to be bred with the likes of Ben's fine animal. Coe went out the front door of the Bulls Head, pistol in hand, and shot twice at the stray, sending the mutt howling in terror. "Shoot at me, will ya," Wild Bill raged in an attempt to influence any witnesses into thinking that Coe's shots were intended for the marshal. Quicker than the eye could blink, Hickok had just shot once from each revolver. One .36 caliber slug tore into Coe's midsection, slamming him into the dirt street. Marshal Hickok's deputy sheriff, Mike Williams, who had heard Coe's shots at the stray dog was in the process of coming on the scene to investigate. Hickok heard Williams' thundering footsteps on the boardwalk behind him. Wild Bill, who later stated that he feared it was Ben Thompson sneaking up from behind to ambush him, whirled around with both Colt pistols blazing their second shots. Deputy Mike Williams was blasted and catapulted through the window of the Alamo Saloon that Hickok had exited. Mike William's life expired on the spot and Phil Coe later followed. The citizens of Abilene had had enough. To kill a scoundrel who lived his life off street fillies and in dives could be tolerated. But to kill a good town citizen and family man, the likes of well-respected Mike Williams, was too much.

The citizens of Abilene had learned what the citizens of Hays City had realized—that Wild Bill Hickok was not the great well, admired lawman the eastern dime novel writers told about. In fact, it became quite obvious that Hickok is a trigger-happy paranoid gunman who shoots first and doesn't even ask questions later. And as with Hickok's killings in Hays City when he was marshal there, Abilene citizens concluded that Wild Bill was using his lawman badge to settle his own personal problems. No, the killer marshal who spent his waking hours lurching in the haunts and dives, was not the one to be the law for the good town folk of Abilene, Kansas. Wild Bill and his ole buddy Joe were given fair warning by the vigilantes: "Remove yourselves from Dickerson County DIE-rectly or there will be a double hangin' at sunup."

Ben Thompson was hoping for the lynching but Hickok and California Joe as usual, to avoid retaliation, disappeared into the darkness of night.

Ben ends his story with his favorite saying, "That Hickok needs a killin."

"We aim to see to it," Kidd remarks to Ben as the seven Irish Avengers ride out of Abilene.

Kidd returns to Indian trading with Willowee, and the six other Irishmen return to their duties. Where Wild Bill Hickok and California Joe go for a while is anyone's guess.

What any civilians or soldiers think of Wild Bill as a lawman, there is no disputing that he is a deadly gunologist. For in the span of just two years 1869 to 1871, form the short distance of Hays City to Abilene, Kansas.

HICKOK'S SCORE:

3 Civilians	Dead
1 U.S. Cavalry Soldier	Dead
1 U.S. Cavalry Soldier	Wounded
1 Deputy Marshal	Dead
1 U.S. Cavalry Hound	Dead

Courtesy Of Kansas State Historical Society

Ben Thompson

Courtesy Of Kansas State Historical Society

School Kid John Wesley Hardin And His 2 Guns

CHAPTER EIGHT
ALONG COMES JACK

In the spring of 1873, Lt. Colonel George Custer's 7th Cavalry ends the Kentucky campaign of chasing the Ku Klux clan and the whiskey bootleggers. The joke is that the 7th Cavalry soldiers joined the redneck clan and drank up all the bootleggers' moonshine. George Custer did not think too highly of his 7th Cavalry being used to harass American citizens. George tells General Phil Sheridan, "Why the hell doesn't the government just create a civilian investigation bureau and hire some white house bastard to run it—and let us Army boys do the real work!" Custer's 7th Cavalry is ordered to make their new headquarters at Forts Rice and Lincoln in Dakota Territory.

Kidd Kelly is doing his usual Indian trading and intelligence recon, but while making a trip to the Dakotas, with their covered wagon, Kidd and Willowee have an unfortunate accident. Their wagon flips in a trench and it pins Willowee under it. Willowee breaks a leg in several places. Although Kidd is able to reset the leg in a make-shift cast, the leg fails to heal properly. Willowee can no longer travel without feeling much pain so Kidd must leave her at the Pine Ridge Indian Reservation in Dakota to be with her Miniconious Sioux tribe. Kidd Kelly does not know when he will see Willowee again, for Indian activity on the northern plains is on the rise. Willowee's position, as a companion to Kidd, will not be replaced by another Indian. Willowee had taught Kidd well, over their years of travel, graduating him into an ace of knowledge in Indian languages, signs and habits. Kidd Kelly's replacement partner, at his own request to General Phil Sheridan is a young Army soldier who is kin to the Kelly clan. He is Jack Kelly, Jr., son of Kidd's older brother Jack Senior, and the Irish prostitute who were both killed in the draft riots of New York City during the U.S. Civil War.

Jack Jr., now about nineteen years of age, had joined the U.S. Army two years earlier in hope of coming out west to hook up with his uncle and cousins. Jack is of small stature but with well-muscled arms and powerful vice-grip hands, from two years of duty as an Army blacksmith. This condition allowed him to achieve the arm wrestling championship of the U.S. Cavalry and the dub "THE ANVIL". Jack "The Anvil" Kelly displays a mean look with his shaved head and trimmed beard. For being a splendid blacksmith, Kidd tags him "Black Jack". Black Jack, being a New York City Dead Rabbits Gangster, joins the 7th Cavalry Irish Avengers and is anxious to avenge the killing of John Kelly.

Late into 1873, Kidd and Black Jack hear that Wild Bill Hickok has joined and is traveling with, Buffalo Bill Cody's Wild West Show. The show is traveling through the eastern cities of the United States and the Kellys can only hope that the show comes their way, so they can stage a Wild West Show of an Irish flavor. Early in the year 1874, Kidd Kelly and nephew Black Jack hatch plans to make a hit on Wild Bill Hickok, even though Hickok is in the east performing for Buffalo Bill's Wild West Show. The show is scheduled to stop in New York City for a performance. The Kelly's telegraph boyhood buddies and fellow Dead Rabbits gang members who are now attached to the dreaded Irish WHYOS gang of New York City. The message that the Kelly's in the 7th Cavalry sends is:

"If and when Buffalo Bill's show appears in New York, dump Wild Bill in the city sewers with a rabbit cadaver."

However, Buffalo Bill Cody, who has friends with connections in the U.S. Army, receives word that Wild Bill Hickok is poison for the Wild West Show with the 7th Cavalry and that Krazy Kelly vendetta on Hickok's head. Buffalo Bill advises Hickok to catch a train to parts unknown, and the Kellys lose out on another chance to avenge John Kelly.

The summer of 1874 sees George Custer's 7th Cavalry discover gold in the Black Hills of South Dakota. When the civilian population gets word of the discovery, the stampede is on, despite the fact that it is in Indian Territory. Prospectors pour in from all parts of the United States, Canada, Mexico and from across the oceans. General Sheridan attempts to control the surge, but to no avail. Camp towns start popping up all over the Black Hills, with the main camp being called Deadwood. The 7th Cavalry sets up a camp of their own and name it Custer City. The gold fever is drawing in prospectors, investors, businessmen and service people of all kinds to help build the camp towns and mining operations. The rush is also sucking in gamblers, swindlers, claim jumpers, thieves, murderers, shady women and any other two-bit hustler looking for a fast take—just the kind of action for the tastes of Wild Bill Hickok and his shadow, California Joe. But Hickok and Joe ain't suicidal. No way are they showing up in the Black Hills just so they can get buried there by the **RABID IRISHMEN OF THE 7**TH **CAVALRY.**

Late in 1875, the command at Fort Lincoln, Dakota Territory assigns a U.S. Army Indian scout to assist Kidd and Jack Kelly in their reconnaissance of the Sioux and Cheyenne. His Indian name is "Chagoo Hurpa". It doesn't take the Kellys long to realize that this Indian scout will be nothing but trouble as well as totally useless in their recon. When the scout goes out on patrol ahead of the Kellys, he seems to somehow "get lost" and when he finally does return, he never fails to be all drunk up on corn alcohol and/ or peyote. What takes the cake is when Kidd and Black Jack stop off at the Pine Ridge Reservation with their new scout to look in on Willowee. What she informs them, kind of shakes them up a bit. Willowee tells them that "Chagoo Hurpa" in English means "broken penis".

"Broken Penis?" Black Jack gulps, "That's just great! We are being led about the country by some Indian named after an inoperative male sex organ!"

"He's outta here!" Kidd barks.

"Yeah," Black Jack says while looking at Willowee and nodding his head towards his Uncle Kidd. "We don't need anymore 'pricks' in this outfit."

"Mind your lip, boy, you're in the company of a lady." Kidd growls as his face turns red from embarrassment of being "taken" by the boys at Fort Lincoln.

Black Jack and Willowee chuckle aloud in unison as Kidd storms back to his horse to grab a bottle of Irish whiskey from the saddlebag. After a good long guzzle, Kidd howls, "Just wait 'till I get ahold a those guys back at Lincoln and we'll see who's got the 'broken penis!'" After another good gulp of firewater, Kidd hands the bottle to Jack and can't keep from joining in on Jack and Willowee's hideous laughter. It's all just a harmless joke but just the same Kidd and Black Jack return to duty minus Chagoo Hurpa.

Official List	Date of Enlistment		Data
Long Bear: *Coonough Tikuchris*	A	May 9	On D.S. at Yellowstone Depot since June 15.
Black Porcupine: *Sami Cotis*	A	May 9	On D.S. at Ft. Lincoln since May 17.
Climbs The Bluff: *Teru Chitt Honochs*	A	May 9	Carrying dispatches in the field since June 1.
Curly Head: *Pichga Ri Ni*	A	Apr. 27	Carrying dispatches in the field since June 22.
Horn In Front: *Arrin Quis Coo*	A	May 9	On D.S. at Yellowstone Depot since June 15.
One Horn: *Achno Arricas*	A	May 9	On D.S. at Ft. Lincoln since May 17.
Laying Down: *Sita Wara*	A	May 9	On D.S. at Ft. Lincoln since May 17.
Owl: *Horr*	A	May 13	On D.S. at Ft. Lincoln since June 17.
Wagon: *Sapararu*	A	May 13	On D.S. at Ft. Lincoln since June 17.
Broken Penis: *Chagoo Hurpa*	D	Nov. 13 '75	D at Ft. Lincoln
Cards	D	Nov. 13 '75	D at Ft. Lincoln
Left Hand: *Quigh Chwi*	D	Dec. 9 '75	D at Ft. Lincoln
Sticking Out: *Bo In E Naga*	D	Dec. 11 '75	D at Ft. Lincoln
The Shield: *Waha Chumka*	D	Dec. 11 '75	D at Ft. Lincoln
Round Wooden Cloud: *Machpa Gachumga*	X	Mar. 31	Sioux
Bear Come Out: *Mato Hinapa*	X	Feb. 3	Sioux
White Cloud: *Machpa A Cha - Mahpia Sha*	X	May 14	Sioux
Bear Running In The Timber: *Matochun Way A Ga Mun*	X	May 11	Sioux
William Cross	X	Apr. 17	Half Sioux
William Jackson	+	June 25	¼ Pikuni
William Baker	+	May 4	Half Ree
Robert Jackson	D	Dec. 25 '75	¼ Pikuni

Note Chagoo Hurpa

CHAPTER NINE
ANNIHILATION

Spring of 1876, some two years into the Black gold rush, Kidd Kelly hears that Wild Bill Hickok has gotten married to Agnes Lake Thatcher, the bedlam circus owner who had come to Hays City, Kansas, those years ago when Wild Bill was the marshal there. It seems that Hickok had no choice but to take this desperate action to keep himself out of the gutters of life. Ever since he shot and killed his own deputy in Abilene, Kansas, Wild Bill has been unable to obtain any type of law enforcement position. Word is that "Wild Bill Hickok can't get a job guardin' sheep". Being unable to pan for gold in the rich deposits of the Black Hills, for fear of the Irishmen of the 7th Cavalry, Hickok tries his hand at pannin' out the old fresh widow of over 10 years his senior. Talley is that Wild Bill is settling down somewhere back east with his bride. It now looks to the Kelly's that their chances are gettin' mighty slim to *get* Hickok.

On June 25th, Kidd and Black Jack are a two-day ride from Little Big Horn of Montana Territory where George Custer's 7th Cavalry attempted to take on the entire nations of the Sioux and Cheyenne Indians. When the Kelly's and other soldiers come upon the battlefield, following the battle, they discover that George and his entire Cavalry are wiped out, horses included, except for one. Soldiers had shot their own horses to lay down for shields. Most all of Custer's men are either scalped, castrated, quartered or mutilated in some way.

Knowing through experience that not all of the over 250 soldiers could have been instantly killed, Kidd knows that any of Custer's wounded had to have been tortured to death after the battle. For some reason, however, George Custer's body had not been molested, except for small sticks driven into his eardrums. George has one bullet hole in this chest and one through his head. Now, Tom Custer's body is a whole different sight. He can only be identified by his tattoos. Tom's body has not only been scalped, but he was also castrated with his torso cut open from neck to crotch. His inners are strewn about like spaghetti.

The slain 7th Cavalry soldiers have to be buried or covered up on the spot due to the flesh getting ripe in the summer sun and heat and with wolves, coyotes and buzzards running or flying off with severed body parts. At this time it is unknown if any of Custer's men were taken prisoner, though it is highly improbable. Kidd Kelly thinks to himself that maybe this battle could have turned out otherwise if George Custer had not always been in such a rush to seek the glory of "being there first". Custer's 7th was assigned two rapid-fire, high velocity Gatling guns that are capable of firing hundreds of rounds per minute. These two weapons surely would have cut down many of the enemy and maybe allowed time for reinforcements to arrive. But no, George refused the heavy artillery, stating that moving the weapons would slow down his Cavalry. George had always desired the quick and deadly surprise attack, to the point that he ordered his soldiers not to carry their Cavalry sabers. George Custer liked to charge down on Indian villages just before sunup, while most Indians were still sleeping. George feared that the clanging sound made by the sabers slapping against the horse saddles when the Cavalry was on the charge, would serve as an alarm clock.

When General Phil Sheridan receives the report that George Custer's 7th Cavalry was completely wiped out at Little Big Horn and that the Indians killed any wounded, he puts out an order for a Sioux and Cheyenne campaign, with silent demands to annihilate any and all Indians that were involved in the battle.

Not only is the remainder of the entire 7th Cavalry to be involved, but also the 9th Cavalry and the U.S. Army 14th Infantry. Now not all of the Irish Avengers or Dead Rabbits gangsters in the entire 7th Cavalry were wiped out at Little Big Horn. Kidd and Black Jack Kelly are still around and only one Kelly, Patrick, is reported to be killed at the battle. With many of the new recruits that replaced Custer's men being Irishmen, there is no problem with finding more soldiers to join the sect of Avengers. In fact, so many soldiers of other nationalities want vengeance for Little Big Horn, that a new group is formed that calls themselves:

CUSTER AVENGERS.

Custer Avengers are made up of Irishmen, Germans and others wanting in to avenge their kin or friends being killed by the Sioux. Joining the group from the Army's 14th Infantry is Kelly clansman, Billy Kelly, along with New York City Dead Rabbits, Billy "Lance" Gentles, "Pyro" Tommy O'Ryan and the female who still masquerades as a man, Katherine "Snags" Shannahan.

Tommy O'Ryan, with his craze to play with explosives, had gone with General Sherman's Army near the end of the Civil War in "Sherman's March to the Sea". O'Ryan made tommybombs by placing a wicked stick of dynamite that was sealed in a metal tube and placed in the center of a sealed can of turpentine. The bomb could be lit and thrown at any intended target. tommybombs were used by Sherman's Army to blow up, burn down and level hundreds of southern businesses, homes, military institutions and plantations. O'Ryan made the statement: "Burning the southern plantations was more excitin' and climatic than rapin' the rebel witches who lived in 'em."

All soldiers joining in the sect of the Custer Avengers obtain tattoos of a skull over crossed sabers with the number of their individual units just out the top of the skull, these being a seven, a nine or the number fourteen. But only the Irish soldiers' number is colored in green. Others are colored black. The Custer Avengers swear an oath that they be a secret sect. But these Custer Avengers won't be too secret. They are about to embark on a 14-year bloody trail of vengeance that won't be too hard to follow.

To assist the Custer Avengers in their quest to track, capture, interrogate and then destroy those Indians that were involved at Little Big Horn, the U.S. Army hires on two of the most deadly man-trackers alive. Their eagle eyes, night-owl ears and hound dog noses can pinpoint any Indian for miles around.

The Irishmen of these two man-trackers is given the position "Chief of Scouts", through the recommendation of Kidd Kelly. This man has a bone to pick with the Oglala Sioux Indians. Not because of Little Big Horn, but because he is the cousin to the husband of Fanny Wiggins Kelly, Josiah Kelly. With Josiah now being disabled and unable to redeem vengeance for Little Mary Kelly, this Chief of Scouts feels bloody obligated to do so. This Irish Tracker's name is Luther S. Kelly.

Luther had moved from the Finger Lakes area of New York, as a youngster, to be near his cousin Black Jack, in New York City. Luther is a Dead Rabbits gangster, but did not go to the Tombs Prison and was too young to join the Union Army for the Civil War. Luther did join the Army near the end of the war and came west with his outfit. When Luther's hitch was up, he loved the west so much that he stayed living in the western wilderness along the Yellowstone River, to learn the ways of nature and the fine art of survival. He once killed and ran off several wolves with the hind-leg of a mule deer he had been quartering. The big, rugged, muscled, mustached, mountain Irishman with hands as big as a grizzly's, is shellacked by the Kelly clan, "Yellowstone".

Yellowstone Kelly's partner, man-tracker and his mentor for a few years while living along the Yellowstone River, is the most prolific Indian killer known to the U.S. Army. He himself had waged a twenty-year, one-man vendetta against the Crow Indian Nation for their torture, murder and mutilation of his pregnant Indian wife. He had been manufacturing liquor at his cabin and trading it to the Crow. While he was away from his cabin for a while to hunt, several Crow Indians came to call. His wife refused to give them whiskey with her husband away. The Indians killed her and carved out the baby from her womb, because they didn't think she should have married a white man. When the white man returned to his cabin, he found two of the Crow Indians who had done the carnage, passed out in the shed from drinking the powerful moonshine. He tied one Indian to a shed post as he slashed out the other Indian's liver, to eat it in the face of the shackled one. He then let the tied-up Indian go free, to warn his Crow Nation that

I'll be a-comin' in vengeance to do all Crow Indians what was done to my family.

This large Scotsman, with red beard and hollowed eyes, was born John Johnston. The soldiers who knew of Johnston's reputation branded him the "Liver Eater". The Indians that escaped the wrath of the Liver Eater, called him "ABSAROKA-DAPIEK" (Crow Killer). Kidd Kelly dubbed this granddaddy of U.S. serial killers and a one-man juggernaut right out of a Scottish castle, "The Master Avenger".

This Master Avenger, Absaroka Dapiek, John Johnston, had armored himself and his huge horse, with two to three-inch thick strips of tree bark, to ward off Indian spear and arrow attacks. For weapons, this Liver Eater carried a .50 caliber rifle, two sawed-off shotguns, a crossbow that could launch an arrow twice as fast and far as any Indian bow, a double-bladed axe and an assortment of knives and daggers. Included in his arsenal, Absaroka Dapiek packs two of the heaviest and most powerful handguns in the world, that are capable of firing a rifle cartridge: the .44 caliber Colt Dragoon. To cart Liver Eater, his armor and his arsenal around is an 1800-pound beast of burden from his Scottish homeland, called a Clydesdale.

There is just one small problem with hiring on John Johnston, the Crow Killer. The U.S. Army has been using Crow Indians to scout against the Sioux and Cheyenne. George Custer had used Crow to scout. So it is the U.S. Army that is able to finally make peace between Absaroka Dapiek and the Crow Nation. And the Crow are more than happy to oblige, before the Master Avenger renders the Crow an endangered species. The Liver Eater is content with the Army invitation for new fish to fry, and he sets his appetite toward to a Sioux and Cheyenne menu. "I've been livin' like a wolverine for the past 20 years," Johnston cracks. "Runnin' from prey to prey, never sleepin' in the same hole twice. Sure gonna be swell to run with a pack."

Both Yellowstone Kelly and John Johnston obtain tattoos of skull and sabers. Yellowstone's number is painted Irish green. Absaroka Dapiek's is painted blood red.

During the weeks following the Little Big Horn battle, the Custer Avengers, with the aid of their two new scouts, pounce down on many small bands of Sioux and Cheyenne. Kidd and Black Jack will never forget witnessing Absaroka Dapiek do his culinary craft. When a band of Indians are captured and prepared for interrogation by the Avengers, one Indian would be tied to a tree and left to live, so he could spread the word to the Indian Nations of what sight he sees. Johnston then forces another Indian to swallow a large amount of raw alcohol. The Liver Eater continues on by slicing open the victim's stomach to allow the alcohol to flow out freely. The flowing alcohol is set afire by Johnston, to cook the Indian's inners. Once the Indian is cooked alive, to Johnston's liking, he slashes out the liver that has been sauteed in the victim's au jus, so to devour it in the face of the surviving Indian. Although the Custer Avengers do not flinch at watching Absaroka Dapiek's barbecue, none accept the Liver Eater's kind offer to join in the feast. And Kidd Kelly prefers his liver with onions. Johnston's tactics definitely get the Indians to talk about what had occurred at the battle of Little Big Horn.

The Custer Avengers learn that once the battle had ended, the Indian braves removed the weapons from the battlefield, and then let the Indian women and children in to have some fun. They tortured Custer's wounded and hacked up their bodies with knives and axes. Some wounded soldiers were dragged around by horse while the Indian kids chased after, to jump aboard the soldiers so to stomp out blood and breath.

An account is told by the interrogated Indians of why George Custer was not mutilated, except for his ears. The Indians claim that George Custer committed suicide by shooting himself in the head after the Indians shot him in the chest. Indians see suicide as a weakness and no Indian brave wanted his scalp for fear of being cursed by an evil spirit that might cause them to do the same. It was Indian women who drove wooden sewing awls into George's eardrums, so he could hear the needs of the Indian better in his next life.

Now Captain Tom Custer is a different tale. It is told by Indian eye-witnesses that Tom had put up a brave and fierce fight while taking many arrow and bullet hits. It's told that the Indian, Rain in the Face, cut out Tom's heart and liver, to eat them in revenge for Captain Tom arresting and beating the Indian on an earlier occasion. some other Indians, however, think Rain in the Face did it to gain the strength of a great warrior.

There is another tale told by some of the Indian women who were there, that at least two of Custer's soldiers were actually women with short hair heads. One was found dead but the other was only wounded. She was raped by Sioux braves, until her throat was cut. So many of Custer's soldiers had their sex organs chopped up or off, that it could have been overlooked that some soldiers were women.

One of the Indian women being questioned by the Custer Avengers shouts out in English, for all to hear, "It was the finest hour of the Oglala Sioux and the greatest warrior Chief Crazy Horse."

"And who the hell may you be," Kidd Kelly questions, "to be bestowing that honor to Crazy Horse?"

"I am the woman of Crazy Horse," she answers, "and all Oglala know he is the greatest."

"Well, I am sure Mister Crazy Horse has many women." Kidd says to prick her. "Now, us Kelly's sure appreciate learning who you Oglala's honor as your greatest. For we too will honor him some day in an Irish tradition and when that day comes, it will be the finest hour of the spirit of Mary Kelly, God rest her soul."

When General Phil Sheridan receives the Custer Avengers' report on what occurred to Custer's wounded, *the only god west of the Mississippi*, who once stated, "If you destroy the buffalo, you destroy the means by which the Indian lives, and what good is a buffalo for except for slaughter," now adds, "It's high time to consider the Sioux and Cheyenne red buffalo for slaughter."

Note: Top of 4th column of Tribune News shows that "there was" a survivor of Custer's 7th Cavalry of the Little Big Horn Battle. But since he was only a Crow Indian scout, the Tribune wrote that he was plausible.

-See Next Page-

FIRST ACCOUNT OF THE CUSTER MASSACRE

TRIBUNE EXTRA

Price 25 Cents.

BISMARCK, D. T., JULY 6, 1876.

MASSACRED

GEN. CUSTER AND 261 MEN THE VICTIMS.

NO OFFICER OR MAN OF 5 COMPANIES LEFT TO TELL THE TALE.

3 Days Desperate Fighting by Maj. Reno and the Remainder of the Seventh.

Full Details of the Battle.

LIST OF KILLED AND WOUNDED

Bismarck Tribune's Special Correspondent Slain.

Squaws Mutilate and Rob Dead.

Victims Captured Alive Tortured.

What Will Congress Do About It?

Shall This Be the Beginning of the End?

**U.S. Soldier, Stripped, Filleted, Castrated
And Disemboweled By Indians**

Courtesy Of Kansas State Historical Society

Yellowstone Kelly

John
"Liver Eater"
Johnston

CHAPTER TEN
OPERATION DUCK BILL

In the last week of July 1876, just one month after George Custer's 7th Cavalry was wiped out, Kidd Kelly and nephews Black Jack and Yellowstone receive information which amazingly surprises them. Wild Bill Hickok and his sidekick, California Joe, had come to the Black Hills of the Dakota Territory. The word is that the two are making camp in Deadwood. Kidd had been thinking that he might never have the opportunity to cross paths with Hickok again, unless he quit the Army life to track him down. Kidd now figures that Hickok and Joe must be thinking that with George Custer's 7th Cavalry now out of the way, the Hays City confrontation is now all forgotten and the rabid Irishmen of the 7th are terminated. Wild Bill Hickok has gotten married in the month of March, and it looked to some that he was changing his "wild" ways and settling into a sedentary way of life.

BUT NO! There will be white black birds before Wild Bill Hickok alters his true character. The lure to now get in on the action of the boozing, gambling, whoring life of Deadwood is too great to keep Hickok at his new bride's side. Yes, Hickok's character of not lasting long in anything he does in life carries on. But how long will Hickok last in Deadwood?

The Kellys intend to see Deadwood as the wall that puts a stop to Hickok's wandering ways. The Kelly's of Kidd, Black Jack, Yellowstone and Billy, along with Kidd's boyhood buddies, Lance Gentles, Snags Shannahan and Tommy O'Ryan, all receive permission to take a temporary leave from the U.S. Army's Sioux and Cheyenne Campaign, so to travel to Deadwood and avenge soldier John Kelly and the honor of the 7th Cavalry. Although General Phil Sheridan's unwritten law to bring in Hickok dead or alive, is still valid, the seven Avengers are not to make it look as if it's a U.S. Army operation. Wild Bill Hickok is too well known and if he were to be assassinated, it will cause for much publicity. It is not to look to the politicians back east that Sheridan's Army is going about the west killing American citizens—especially one who looks to some as an American West hero. The seven Irish Avengers discard all clothing and equipment displaying U.S. Army logos and don themselves up as gold prospectors wearing Levi jeans and overalls. Each is bringing along their .50 caliber Army issue rifle and Colt .45 Peacemaker revolver. These soldiers are not going to be outgunned in Deadwood, as the Kelly's were that day back in Tommy Drum's Saloon, when John Kelly was killed. As they prepare their horses with civilian saddles for their destination, Kidd Kelly shows the six others photographs of Wild Bill Hickok and California Joe, so to familiarize any who may not have ever laid eyes on the Prince of the Pistoleers and King of the Riflemen. Snags Shannahan cracks aloud, "Yea, I can see why someone would call Hickok 'Duck Bill'." Seven Irish gangsters from New York City, who now reside in General Sheridan's U.S. Army of the West, and seeking vengeance for fellow Dead Rabbiteer, John Kelly, haul out for Deadwood, South Dakota, in:

Operation Duck Bill.

To initiate their directive once the seven Irish Gangsters arrive into Deadwood, South Dakota, during the last week of July 1876, they set up a campsite on the outskirts of town. Once settled in, to go about as gold prospectors, they divide into two teams. Kidd, with nephews Black Jack and Yellowstone, make up a trio. Billy Kelly and his 14th Infantry troopers of Gentles, O'Ryan and Shannahan form a foursome. Both squads are to survey Deadwood's saloons, gambling halls, dives and haunts to gather up intelligence on Wild Bill Hickok's activities, habits and associates. They will reunite back in camp at sundown to discuss their reconnaissance.

With the first day of recon, the Kellys learn that Wild Bill Hickok has a campsite of his own at the opposite end of Deadwood, in an area known as White Wood Gulch. This is a place known to house the rowdy element about Deadwood and the local prostitutes known as "The Soiled Doves of Hells Half Acre". Wild Bill camps there in a canvas-covered wagon, alongside tents of his sidekick California Joe and two brothers known as Colorado Charlie Utter and Steve Utter. Colorado Charlie is an Indian trader that, according to Sioux Indians who were interrogated by the Custer Avengers, had been trading repeating rifles to the Sioux. The weapons given to the Sioux by Utter were used to kill Custer's men at Little Big Horn. The seven Avengers debate taking down all of Hickok's group, but to do so could expose the gang of Army soldiers. Although the Kellys have sworn an oath to the U.S. Army, their vow to fellow Dead Rabbits takes precedence over Army matters. Wild Bill Hickok had been the elusive nemesis of the Kellys for some six years now, making him the prime objective over the Utters' illegal trading of firearms. And Kidd Kelly thinks that Charlie Utter could be used to set up Hickok, if Utter were to fear that the U.S. Army could hang him for his illegal trading of contraband rifles to Indians.

The Avenger's second day of recon yields information that Wild Bill Hickok and California Joe, on a daily basis, headquarter at a saloon on the main street of Deadwood, called the Number Ten Saloon. The Number Ten is a long narrow saloon, crudely made of large, long Black Hills pine logs and with a sawdust covered floor. There is a pine plank bar on wooden barrels in the front of the saloon, by the only door to the outside and a couple of card tables in the rear of the building. There are windows in the front wall looking onto Main Street, but no windows in the sidewalls due to the other buildings being attached to both sides. There is no back door to go out the rear of the Number Ten, *but* there is an open archway in the sidewall near the card tables, that leads into the building next door, which is called The Bella Union Dance Hall. The Bella Union is not in use during the daytime hours, but the archway has no doors so it is open at all times. After sundown, when prospectors and miners are through working the gold claims, the Bella Union livens up with drinking, gambling, pool shooting and dance hall girls operating at full throttle. The open archway is available for customers to wander to and from the two establishments without having to venture outside and into the weather—especially the Black Hills harsh winters.

The Bella Union Dance Hall is over twice the width of the Number Ten Saloon and it too is made of pine log walls and roofing with added log posts to hold up its wider ceiling. The dance hall also has its sawdust covered dirt floor. There are windows only in the front wall next to doors leading out onto Main Street. There is a bar in the front of the dance hall and a large wooden dance stage in the center of the building with seventeen curtain-closing booths surrounding it. Dance hall girls called "Fairy Bellas" use the curtain-closing booths to privately entertain their customers. There are also gaming and billiard tables about. Just as with the Number Ten, the Bella Union relies on wood-burning stoves, oil lamps and candles to heat and light its dark interior. For fire safety, of course, the Bella's are not lit during the day when the hall is not in use. On the other side of the Bella Union is a small diner, about the same size as the Number Ten Saloon, but instead of an archway, it has a small door in the sidewall for an entrance into the Bella Union, besides its own front door to the boardwalk on Main Street. This diner calls itself "Crumbs of Comfort Along the Crack in the Wall".

The Kellys visit the Bella Union during its operating hours and find that when standing in the dance hall, they can observe through the archway, anyone playing cards in the rear of the Number Ten. But during the daytime, when the Bella is dark, they find that anyone playing cards in the Number Ten would not see anyone standing deep in the shadows of the Bella Union. And with the dance hall being unoccupied during the daytime, assassins could easily hide and wait for anyone who could be set up to play cards in the Number Ten. The plan for the hit on Wild Bill Hickok is now obvious to the Kellys: wait for Hickok to be playing cards in the Number Ten during the day, when most miners and prospectors are busy working their claims, and gun him down while hiding in wait, in the day-time, in the dark Bella Union.

In order to get away cleanly with assassinating Wild Bill Hickok and not drawing attention to the U.S. Army soldiers being involved, as General Sheridan insists, the Kelly's need a "fall guy". And the luck of the Irish shines upon the Kellys when the appearance of that fall guy comes their way. While checking out the saloons and dives about town, the trio of Kellys make the acquaintance of a Deadwood dive-bomber whom Kidd thinks is one of the mangiest looking characters that he has ever gazed upon. With his crossed eyes and crooked nose, he wears a floppy worn out sombrero, with shirt and trousers to match. Tucked down into the waistband of his ragged trousers that are held up by suspenders made of rope, is a rusty looking cap and ball revolver. Tied to a ring on the handle butt of this revolver is a long rawhide lasso that loops around the neck of this Deadwood Boogeyman, who calls himself Jack McCall.

After the Kellys share their bottle of whiskey with this down-and-out character, at the bar of the Number Ten Saloon, he mentions that he frequently plays poker with a Wild Bill Hickok. But McCall is fed up with this Hickok "gypping me outta my purse". McCall drunkenly brags to the Kellys that he would kill the cheat Hickok, if he thought he could get away with it. With this remark by McCall, the Kelly's hustle him out of the Number Ten Saloon, into the night-time crowded Bella Union Dance hall, and into a private curtained booth, with of course, a fresh bottle of whiskey to boot. This Jack McCall is just the type of jackleg character that the Kellys are looking for—a loser who has been drifting about, hoping to find his niche in life. This is someone who wants to do a deed in life that would make himself look important. This is a character who would do most any task to have a few dollars to pay for the noxious triple W's: "Whiskey, Wagering and Wile Women". Yes, Jack McCall perfectly fits the profile and the Kellys know he could quite easily be set up for the kill of Wild Bill.

Black Jack Kelly tells McCall that the three Irishmen would like to see Hickok dead, because Hickok had gunned down their kin in Hays City, Kansas. The three Kellys assure McCall that they have the power and influence to back up and reward him if he were to kill Wild Bill. And if McCall were to be charged with a crime, they could get him cleared and sent down the road. Jack McCall now swears that he can and will accomplish the risky deed.

Kidd tells McCall to keep cool for a while, until "we tree'im for the kill". The Kellys and McCall shake hands on the deal, causing McCall to notice their tattoos of skull and sabers on their right forearms.

"Ya'll belong to some kinda club?" McCall quips.

"Yea," Yellowstone returns. "Death to those who tread on us or renege on their word."

"You ain't gotta worry about me," McCall comes back. "My word's good as gold."

Kidd tells McCall to grab the whiskey bottle and the Kellys tow him off to the Irishmen's campsite, so to introduce him to the foursome of the 14th Infantry. After introductions, Lance Gentles, the senior of these Dead Rabbits, questions Kidd on the side. "Ya know you can't trust a Limey," Lance states, referring to Jack McCall being an Englishman.

"We got no choice, iffen we want to get Hickok," Kidd answers.

McCall is kept overnight, but come tomorrow, McCall's anxiousness to become a famous figure in the world of western gunfighters, almost blotches any Kelly plans to knock out Wild Bill Hickok. Wild Bill took the winnings from that game, and is already into a higher stakes poker game at the Number Ten Saloon. Jack McCall is grumbling to his glass of beer that Kidd has bought him, on how that was the last time that Hickok will ever "cheat me out of my stakes". McCall, drunk as usual, and now feeling cocky with his Kelly backup buddies alongside, decides to wander over to the card tables and look in on the play. Kidd signals to Black Jack to keep on McCall's heels.

McCall walks up behind where Hickok is sitting at the card table and leers into the game. Wild Bill is unaware of McCall, because there are many patrons lingering about. Suddenly, without any type of warning to Black Jack, McCall starts to pull his revolver that is tucked down in his pants. Black Jack is caught off guard, but McCall being drunk, is slow in his action, allowing Black Jack time to halt McCall from finishing his move. It is not the time to be shooting Hickok, because McCall is too drunk to pull it off successfully, and there are too many witnesses about for Black Jack to slip in a shot of his own. Black Jack grabs McCall by the arm and spins him through the archway and into the crowd of the Bella Union, to disappear before anyone notices McCall's foolish actions. But Kidd and Yellowstone had observed McCall's stunt from their position at the Number Ten bar. Kidd and Yellowstone depart the Number Ten through its front door to meet up with Black Jack and McCall on the boardwalk in front of Crumbs of Comfort Diner. Kidd instructs Black Jack to obtain a bottle of whiskey and again escort the fool McCall back to the Irishman's campsite. Kidd now realizes that the Dead Rabbits must strike quickly and tomorrow, before McCall foolishly exposes the gang's plot to do in Hickok and validate Gentles' statement, "you can't trust a Limey".

Dave McCanles Called Him "Duck Bill"

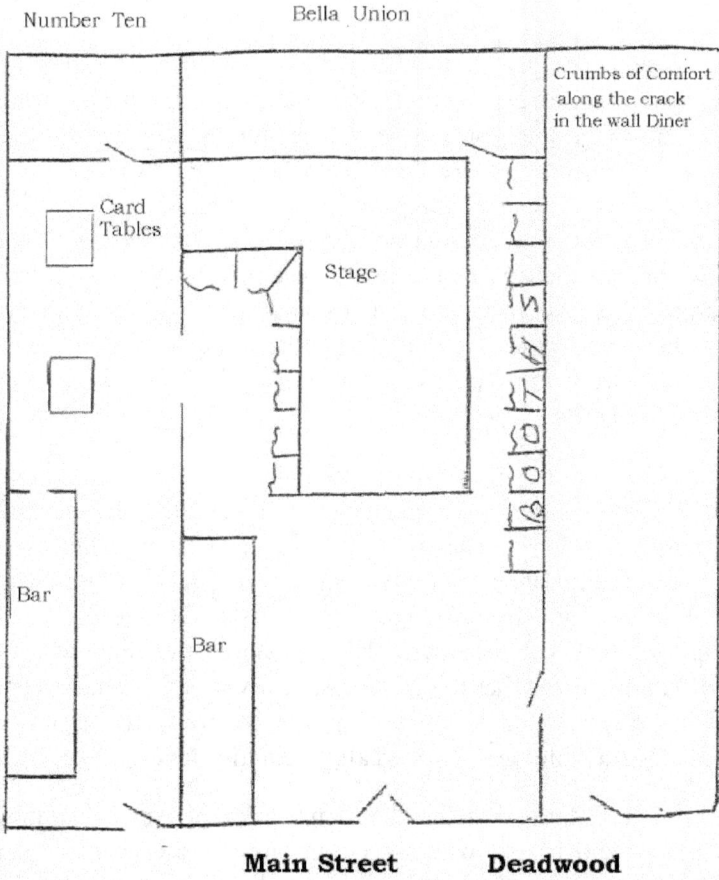

Number Ten   Bella Union

Crumbs of Comfort
along the crack
in the wall Diner

Card
Tables

Stage

Bar

Bar

Main Street   Deadwood

JMR

CHAPTER ELEVEN
SET 'IM UP

First light of August 2nd awakes the seven Irish Avengers in their campsite this history-making day. Jack McCall, who has been kept under wraps by the gang, snoozes away his drunken stupor of the previous night. Kidd, Yellowstone, Gentles, Shannahan and O'Ryan are going over town to stake out Hickok's campsite in White Wood Gulch, while Black Jack and Billy Kelly keep hold on McCall. The five Avengers are just a short while into their surveillance of the gulch and its residents, when California Joe steps out from his tent that is next to Wild Bill's covered wagon. Joe goes to the wagon to awake the Prince of the Pistoleers and together the two begin their usual morning jog downtown for "breakfast from a booze bottle".

The five Avengers now have the opportunity to get to their set-up man, Colorado Charlie Utter, who sleeps late in his tent the other side of Wild Bill's home on wheels. The Irish gang startles Charlie Utter awake by jarring open the entrance flap of his canvas abode. Kidd is surprised to see that Charlie does not sleep alone on his bed of straw. Colorado Charlie has a companion that Kidd at first thinks is a man. But once he gets a better gander, Kidd realizes that the guest is actually a female character of the west who dresses and makes herself up like the men of the territory. This gal with Charlie Utter goes by the call, "Calamity Jane".

Calamity Jane is known by the U.S. Army from the days when the Army hired her to haul freight with a six-team, mule-drawn wagon. Jane has the reputation of being one of the finest bullwhip whackers west of the Mississippi. Rumor has it that Calamity once pulled a fully loaded wagon out of the mud when she strapped on one of the mule harnesses to lead the other five mules out. Some thought Jane was called "Calamity" because she could cause one. Some thought she ran into one and others say she is one.

Kidd Kelly advises this Calamity Jane that it would be good sense for her to haul herself down the road, because they have private matters to discuss with Charlie Utter. Jane stares for a while at Kidd in her "who's gonna make me" attitude, but she soon spots the Irish girl Shannahan, who has rugged looks of her own to match any man's. Snags is swinging a hangman's rope with noose, that she made by intertwining fish-net line. Jane, sensing that she may be in for a *calamity* herself, grabs up her buckskin clothing and charges out of Utter's tent, half naked.

Once Calamity Jane vacates the area, Kidd informs Colorado Charlie that the U.S. Army has enough evidence on his trading illegal firearms to the Sioux Indians, to hang him here and now. Charlie Utter is given only one alternative – Wild Bill Hickok's hyde in exchange for his own. Charlie Utter wastes no time in fully agreeing to do whatever is required to keep his neck from being stretched by Shannahan's rope. Kidd instructs Charlie that he is to get Hickok into the Number Ten Saloon today, just after noontime, with the excuse of a big poker game going on. Utter is to also get California Joe out of town by sending him on some sort of trading mission. With California Joe out of town, the Avengers do not fear anyone else in Deadwood being a problem of resistance. For besides Wild Bill Hickok and his buddy Joe, the Kellys feel that "there ain't enough gunfighter guts in Deadwood to string sausage". And with no civilian law enforcement in town, if any foolish citizen were to venture into the way, the Irish gang of soldiers have brought along enough firepower to "blow'em outta the way". Charlie Utter is warned that he will be under the watchful eye of the Avengers. One false move on his part will result in him being immediately gunned down and then hung, dead or alive. The nervously perspiring Colorado Charlie, swears on his mother to oblige.

Kidd and Yellowstone depart Utter's camp and leave the well-armed soldiers of the 14th Infantry, Gentles, Shannahan and O'Ryan, to keep watch on Charlie Utter's actions. Once back to the Irishmen's camp, Kidd directs Black Jack and Billy Kelly to escort the awakening Jack McCall to the Senate Saloon, which is just up the street from the Number Ten Saloon. They are to keep McCall there, wettin' his whistle, until Kidd shows up with further instructions. Kidd and Yellowstone now begin a leisure stroll to downtown Deadwood.

Just before noon, Wild Bill Hickok and California Joe return to their campsite from their short jaunt to downtown Deadwood. They are met by Charlie Utter who convinces Joe to deliver some horses to Crooke City and earn himself some gold dust. While Utter and Joe prepare the ponies for transport, Hickok goes to his wagon to enjoy a midday nap. It is hard work pumping shot glasses full of whiskey off the bar at the Number Ten.

It is shortly after one o'clock this afternoon when Kidd and Yellowstone enter the Number Ten Saloon through its front door. Besides the bartender being present behind the bar, there are several patrons mingling about. Kidd steps to the bar to order a beer as Yellowstone walks to the unoccupied card table at the rear of the number Ten, that is closest to the open archway. Yellowstone purposely sits in the chair at the table that has its back to the archway. He calls out loud for anyone in the saloon who may be interested in a game of draw poker, as he drops clanging gold nuggets on top of the table. Three men in the saloon accept the stranger Yellowstone's challenge and sit in at the four-chair card table. The bartender weighs out any player's gold and exchanges it for poker chips that are used for wagering, besides coin or paper money. Chips can be re-exchanged when players cash out. Yellowstone's objective in this poker game is to hold his chair, whatever the cost, until Charlie Utter delivers up Wild Bill.

Coming up two o'clock this afternoon, Charlie Utter wakes Wild Bill from his nap, to inform him that he has some extra gold nuggets for the two of them to go to the Number Ten Saloon and have "one hell of a blast". Hickok, who would rather play poker for gold than strain his back panning for it, agrees. Colorado Charlie suggests to Wild Bill that he wear his finest gambler's attire for the big game scheduled at the Number Ten.

While Utter prepares the lamb for the slaughter, the big game goes on in the Number Ten, with other players sitting in when any wipe out.

There are plenty of poker chips and cash on the card table when Charlie Utter delivers Wild Bill through the gates of Hell – the front door of the Number Ten Saloon, Main Street, Deadwood, after two o'clock this afternoon of August 2nd, 1876. Wild Bill Hickok is well dressed for this occasion, with his silver-gray trousers and dark boots. He is wearing a long sleeved white fluffed shirt with a red silk sash around his waist. He does not carry his two well known ivory-handled Colt Navy cap and ball .36 caliber revolvers. Instead, he sports two modern cartridge-loaded pistols of unknown caliber, in shoulder holsters under his armpits. Wild Bill's weapons are covered up with a four pocket gray cloth vest that is held closed by a gold chain with pocket watch. The two top pockets of the vest carry his smoking pipe in one and a tobacco pouch in the other. This well-duked-out hombre is topped off with a silver sombrero. Hickok's undivided attention is towards the card game in the rear, and he gives no attention to Kidd at the bar, as he struts by. If he would have, Wild Bill would have surely recognized the Irishman who had faced him in Tommy Drum's Saloon, when John Kelly was shot down and spit out the vow that some day he would see Hickok when his back wasn't covered. But by habit, Wild Bill's love for a big card game overrides any fear that he may have for being in for an ambush. Charlie Utter tosses a good-size bag of gold nuggets on the bar for the bartender to exchange for chips. Utter gives the tray of tokens to Hickok, as Wild Bill stares into the four players' card game.

It is now the time for Yellowstone Kelly to pull out of the card game with the three other players and leave the "hot seat" for Wild Bill Hickok. Yellowstone has had good fortune in the poker game, and as he gathers up his winnings, he asks the bartender to ring the old school bell that hangs on the wall behind the bar. The bartender obliges and the sound of the bell means "drinks for all in the house".

Wild Bill, who does not know who Yellowstone is but is quite able to recognize a winner, comments, "looks like you're surrendering the lucky seat, fella." Wild Bill Hickok has now settled in the chair that Yellowstone has vacated, to assume his position with his back to the archway.

Charlie Utter sits on a stool, to lean back against the wall, across from Hickok. He is cradling a rifle to put on the pretense that he is guarding Wild Bill's back. As Hickok is dealt out five cards for draw poker, he notices that Yellowstone has left behind a rabbit's foot on the card table.

"You forgot your good luck piece fella!" Wild Bill shouts.

"Ah, you keep it Wild Bill," Yellowstone answers. "Maybe today is your lucky day."

Yellowstone Kelly takes Kidd Kelly's place at the saloon bar near the front door, as Kidd leaves out through the door. Kidd goes to the Senate Saloon where Black Jack and Billy Kelly have been keeping McCall in wait. Kidd tells McCall it is now time for him to do his dastardly deed.

"Just creep up behind Hickok like ya did last night. We'll be ready to back your play this time."

Kidd and Black Jack depart the Senate Saloon after instructing Billy Kelly to escort McCall across the street to the Number Ten, where they will be met by Shannahan, who along with Gentles and O'Ryan, had been following Charlie Utter and Wild Bill downtown, from White Wood Gulch. Billy Kelly and Shannahan are to hold McCall there until they see Charlie Utter come out the front door of the Number Ten. This is to give Kidd and Black Jack time to assume their positions. It is coming up near 3 o'clock this afternoon of August 2^{nd,} when Kidd and Black Jack enter into the Crumbs of Comfort Diner, through its front door on Main Street. There are only two customers sitting at the diner's counter and they are Irishmen Gentles and O'Ryan, who have sent the waitress on an errand, so to assume their positions and secure this location. Kidd and Black Jack slip through the side door of the diner that leads into the Bella Union. They barricade the side door, from the Bella side, with a table so that no one can follow in. The two Kellys work their way quickly but quietly through the darkness of the unlit Bella, skirting around gaming tables until they reach the curtain-closing booths that face the archway to the Number Ten Saloon. The two peer through the archway to view the scene of the Number Ten.

At the card table that is closest to the archway, sits four card players. Wild Bill is still in the chair with his back to the archway. He is smoking his pipe that is giving off an aroma of cherry-tainted tobacco smoke. On Hickok's right at the table sits Charlie Rich. Across from Hickok sits retired riverboat captain, Frank Massie. The fourth player, sitting on Hickok's left is the co-owner of the Number Ten, Carl Mann. Charlie Utter is still on his stool, leaning back against the wall and on Massie's right. The bartender behind the bar is Harry Young. Three men standing at the bar, from saloon front to rear, are: Yellowstone Kelly, then town citizens George Shingle and Con Stapleton. Nine men in all, inside the Number Ten Saloon at this time.

Charlie Utter, who has been restlessly on the alert for Kidd, while sitting on his stool facing Hickok and the open archway, now notices Kidd and Black Jack in the shadow of the unlit dance hall. Kidd nods his head sideways in a silent gesture to Utter, to inform him that it is now time to leave out the front of the Number Ten. Kidd and Black Jack back up deeper into the dance hall and into the curtain-closing booth that faces the archway, before any others notice them. Colorado Utter rises from his stool and stands his rifle against the wall. Utter tells Hickok that he is awful hungry and needs to get something to eat at the Crumbs. Wild Bill nods okay but is too involved in the card game to raise any suspicion of Charlie Utter walking out on him. Charlie Utter walks out the front door of the Number Ten, in betrayal of the man he will later call "my pard", leaving Wild Bill's back unguarded.

Within seconds of Utter's departure, in through the same door staggers the man who has been anxiously awaiting his curtain call – Jack McCall. McCall steps to the bar, next to Yellowstone, to order a drink. Yellowstone flips several .45 caliber cartridges on the bar to cover the cost of McCall's drinks. This is no time for McCall to be tossed out of the Number Ten for lack of booze money, as had happened on previous occasions. Ammunition is scarce in the Black Hills, so some saloons, as does the Number Ten will trade a short glass of alcohol for a loaded shelled bullet. No lead balls.

"Whiskey's twenty-five cents," says McCall. "You sure the bartender 'ill take a bullet?"

"It's a shot for a shot," Yellowstone tells McCall. "If a man pulls a gun on ya, would ya wanna put a slug in 'im, or throw two-bits at 'im?"

"Yea, see what ya mean," says McCall. "Harry, gimme a shot of your best stuff," McCall states as he rolls Yellowstone's bullets toward the bartender.

McCall gulps down two shots and puts the shot glass on the bar and calmly struts down to the card game going on at the back of the saloon. As he gets to the archway, he glances into the darkness of the Bella Union and spots the shadowy figures of Kidd and Black Jack. McCall, now confident, steps into the center of the archway, and turns to face the card table. McCall is standing directly behind Hickok's position, in the heavy tobacco-smoke-filled atmosphere of the Number Ten. McCall as yet, has not drawn no concern from the card players, and Hickok is too occupied with raising the betting of the game to notice any threat to himself.

Wild Bill is heard to comment, "I'd bet my life on this hand."

Jack McCall now nervously draws his revolver from down his trouser waistband. Kidd and Black Jack are behind McCall approximately 15 feet inside the dance hall. Kidd is on McCall's left, and Black Jack is on his right. Kidd is holding his Colt .45 Peacemaker and Black Jack is gripping a smaller caliber pistol for better accuracy and lighter percussion. The Kelly's revolvers are cartridge-loaded pieces, whereas McCall's is a cap and ball. (Cap and ball has the gunpowder lead balls and firing caps, loaded individually.) McCall points his old revolver at the back of Hickok's head. Kidd and Black Jack do the same and fire their weapons at the precise time that McCall snaps his. It all sounds as one large gun blast.

But neither Kidd nor Black Jack detect that McCall's revolver fired. The two Kellys have each fired once and quickly retreat deep into the darkness of the Bella Union to observe what now transpires. All the card players and saloon clientele now look towards the report of the loud gun blast, to observe McCall standing behind Hickok's slumped-over body that rests head down on the card table.

McCall is seen with his pistol in hand, hollering "Take that, you cheatin' Bastard!"

McCall attempts to fire his revolver several times into Wild Bill's body, but the gun is not discharging. The three other players, Carl Mann, Frank Massie and Charlie Rich, have already risen from their chairs, to make a dash for the front door. Massie, who was sitting across from Hickok, is holding his arm with his other hand, while running and yelping, "I've been shot!"

McCall now waves his pistol about, pointing it at the bartender, Harry Young and citizens George Shingle and Con Stapleton, as he demands, "Stay back!"

McCall tries again to fire his gun in the air, to run the three out. Even though McCall's pistol is only snapping, Young, Shingle and Stapleton are not taking the chance to challenge McCall, so all three make their exit out the front door. Now only Yellowstone Kelly, who stands his ground at the bar, remains in the Number Ten Saloon with McCall and Hickok's slumped-over body.

Yellowstone snaps, "Time to chuck ass, Jack!"

As McCall spooks past Yellowstone, to make his escape out the front door of the Number Ten, Kidd and Black Jack enter into the Number Ten from the Bella Union, via the archway. Yellowstone guards the front door as Kidd and Black Jack surround Hickok's slumped-over body. Black Jack pulls a knife from his waistband and plunges it into Wild Bill's body, to make sure Hickok is dead. Firing another gunshot would be heard outside. The knifing actions cause Hickok to fall off the chair and onto the sawdust floor. Kidd stops Black Jack from filleting Wild Bill and instructs him to go after Jack McCall and retrieve McCall's pistol before anyone else can examine it and find it inoperative.

There is now only Kidd and Yellowstone in the Number Ten Saloon, with Wild Bill's body. Kidd looks down at Hickok, to notice that Wild Bill is still gripping the pipe in his left hand and his poker cards in his right. Kidd, being curious to see what Hickok meant when his last words were to bet his life on his hand of cards, pries the five cards from Wild Bill's paralyzed blood-covered hand, but then quickly tosses them on the card table. The bullet that had hit Wild Bill in the back of the head had come out his face, blowing blood and flesh about. Kidd glances at the fanned-out cards on the table to see that the four of the five cards that are not covered in Wild Bill's blood are a pair of aces and a pair of eights. Kidd has no desire to wipe the fifth card clean, to get the identity. If he did, the answer to if Wild Bill had a full house (another ace or eight) would be known. Instead, Kidd bends over to wipe what blood he already had on his hand, onto Hickok's vest. As he does so, he removes the tobacco pouch from one upper pocket.

"You won't be needin' this where your goin', Wild Bill," Kidd cracks. "There be plenty a' free smoke in Hell."

Kidd is about to remove the fine gold watch with chain that adorns Hickok's vest, when he catches sight of a spent bullet lying on the ground in a mixture of blood and sawdust. Kidd ignores the watch to immediately pick up and pocket the slug. Charlie Utter now returns through the front door, followed by the local mortician, Doc Ellis Pierce.

Yellowstone Kelly, seeing the doctor, cracks to Charlie Utter, "That's thinkin' ahead, Utter."

"Lock the door," Kidd shouts at Yellowstone.

Kidd orders Charlie Utter and Ellis Pierce to take control of Hickok's body, wrap it up with a curtain from the Bella Union and take the body to Utter's campsite where Utter is to change Hickok's clothes before any Deadwood citizens can view the body. The knife wounds on Hickok would surely show that McCall had an accomplice.

Utter and Pierce are told by Kidd, as Yellowstone glares by, "Tell a soul and yours will join Hickok's!"

As Kidd and Yellowstone step outside from the Number Ten, after unlocking the front door, they are met by a man on the boardwalk who claims to be a newspaper reporter for the "Black Hills Pioneer". The reporter enquires to what happened.

"Some guy shot and killed Wild Bill Hickok and wounded another," is Kidd's response.

Doc Pierce and Charlie Utter now come out of the Number Ten carrying Hickok's covered body. They place the corpse on a horse drawn wagon that Utter had brought along. Steve Utter is now on the scene so the two Utter brothers take Wild Bill to their campsite in White Wood Gulch.

Doc Pierce talks with the Black Hills reporter as Kidd and Yellowstone walk across the street to join the four Irish soldiers of the 14th Infantry who had kept surveillance on the action. The foursome have in their custodya young man whom Shannahan had "snagged" coming out the front door of the supposedly deserted Bella Union Dance Hall. Neither Kidd nor Black Jack were aware of anyone else being in the dance hall when Hickok was shot. But the Bella is big and dark, with many places to hide, and Kidd and Black Jack didn't have time to check out the 17 curtain-closing booths and still get into their positions before McCall entered the Number Ten Saloon. Kidd looks fiercely at the boy as he inquires to his name and to what he saw. The kid, who is shaking like a willow in the wind, with six mean-looking characters circling him, answers that his name is Peter.

Peter states that he was in the dance hall in the front, looking out the windows to watch his freight wagon that was parked on Main Street, when he heard a loud gun blast that trembled the walls. Peter further states that he fell to the floor to avoid being shot and when he heard no more, he ran out. Kidd notices that the young man is holding a bottle of whiskey behind his back.

Thinking that this is the reason why Peter was sneaking through the Bella Union, Kidd asserts, "Okay, Mister Peter, we'll let ya be. But if ya utter a word about being in there, we'll hunt ya down like a rabid dog."

This crack causes the Irish gang to snicker as Peter stutters, while noticing their eerie tattoos, "Please, sir, I don't know nuttin'."

Kidd, now confident, instructs Peter to go about his business. As Peter tears off, Black Jack returns to join the other six Avengers. Black Jack has Jack McCall's revolver and he explains how McCall had tried to escape by attempting to steal a horse that was tied out the front of the Senate Saloon. But because of the August heat, the owner of the horse had loosened the saddle straps and thrown water on the animal. This caused McCall to fall from the horse, saddle and all, into the mud, horse urine and manure. In doing so, McCall dropped his pistol into the dung puddle.

Some of the Senate Saloon customers, who had already heard from fleeing Number Ten patrons that Jack McCall shot Hickok, captured McCall as he lay in the street. In the confusion, Black Jack was able to retrieve McCall's revolver. Kidd examines McCall's old pistol and finds that it has no firing caps. He puts the weapon to his nose to smell for powder burn, but only detects urine odor from the horse dump that McCall had fallen into.

"Why, the duffer didn't even have a loaded gun!" Kidd cracks, causing the gang to shake their heads in amazement.

Kidd hands the pistol back to Black Jack, with the order, "Destroy it!"

Kidd reaches into his pocket to remove the bloody spent bullet that was near Hickok's head. He identifies it as a .45 caliber slug, flattened by and impregnated with, bone and teeth.

"Well, Nephew," Kidd starts in, in his pricking demeanor as he puts his hand on Black Jack's shoulder. "It's from my shot sure enough. I got Hickok and you missed with your pea-shooter and hit the card player on the other side."

"Ah, maybe so," Black Jack comes back, "but you only paralyzed him. I had to stick his heart to keep it from pumpin' his blood down Main Street."

"Jokin' aside," Yellowstone cuts in, "what are we gonna do about the other card player gettin' shot, Uncle?"

"No problem," Kidd tells the group. "Now that Black Jack got McCall's pistol and I got the slug that done Hickok, we'll pass a rumor to the gullible Deadwood citizens that when McCall shot Wild Bill, the bullet went on to hit Frank Massie. Once McCall's revolver is destroyed, who will ever prove otherwise?"

Kidd now draws out his smoking pipe and the Indian embroidered tobacco pouch that he lifted off Hickok, seeing that the pouch bears the initials "J.B.H".

"One thing that I gotta admire about Wild Bill," Kidd comments. "His taste for fine cherry tobacco."

Kidd packs, lights and inhales his pipe, to blow smoke while he continues on his words of wisdom. "Revenge is glory, boys, and glory feeds the soul. It's been a long six year-a-chewin' on it and it sure feels mighty good to finally swallow."

Kidd pulls out his old gold pocket watch to check the time.

"Hell, I forgot to lift Hickok's fine gold watch off 'im. It had a real nice red ruby stone on it. I'm pretty sure that Utter won't miss gettin' it. But it's comin' up on 4 o'clock, guys, and that's happy hour at the Senate. What say we scuffle on over to drink a toast to the Luck of the Irish and the gunshot made for the honor of Dead Rabbits and the 7th Cavalry."

"Yea," Lance Gentles seconds the motion, "and we'll have a shot of good ole Irish whiskey to another damn Limey wiped out by the Irish!"

Number Ten   Bella Union

Office   Dressing Room   Diner

Card Tables

Rich

Massie X McCall

Wild Bill

Mann

X Black Jack

Kidd X

Stage

X O'Ryan

X Harry Young

X Stapleton

X Shingle

X Gentles

Bar

X Yellowstone

Bar

X Peter

Billy Kelly X   X Shannahan

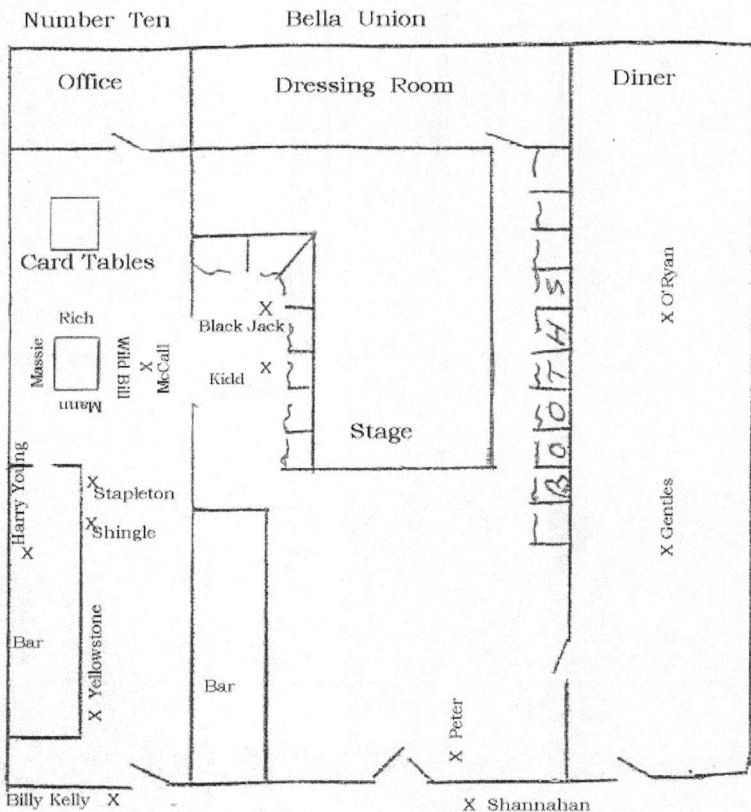

Main Street Deadwood
Who's Who at the Killin'

JMR

Deadwood, 1876

"Calamity Jane" Canary
Courtesy Of Kansas State Historical Society

CHAPTER TWELVE
PLUG UGLIES

The summer's warm morning of August 3, 1876, sets the stage for an audience of residents gawking at the group of eight individuals smartly strutting down Main Street, Deadwood, from their campsite on a hill.

Seven of the group are now out of their worn mining costumes that they used for masquerade during the last week. They now sport half of their four piece eastern city suits from New York, just the pants and vest to go along with their Cavalry boots. For a hat they are wearing their Irish plug uglies.

Without a suit jacket or a shirt, their bare arms dramatically display their loud tattoos. But for obvious reasons, Shannahan has her vest buttoned up.

The eighth individual marching with them is dressed in buckskin pants and boots, also no shirt but wearing a vest made of tree bark to cover his tattooed upper body.

He is John Johnston, the Liver Eater, who had come to Deadwood overnight so to join the wolf pack buddies.

The seven Irish of the lot are each armed with one of two Army issue Colt .45 pistols. Four of the seven shoulder Remington .50 caliber carbines as three others, for some reason, tote wooden spears that dangle three dead rabbits, one on a stick.

The Scotsman Johnston wears his two massive Colt Dragoon revolvers.

This gang of eight is coming to Jack McCall's trial that some Deadwood citizens are attempting to hold in the Bella Union Dance Hall.

The Kellys had struck a deal with McCall and they fully intend to keep to their end of the bargain.

They will make sure through whatever means necessary, that McCall will be found not guilty at this trial, paid off for his troubles, and sent down the road.

And with no civilian law enforcement or gunfighter guts left in Deadwood, who's to stop them?

Before the trial begins, the Kellys strongly remind the jury of its livelihood needs. The jury of gold lovers get the message.

Black Jack Kelly instructs McCall, "The trial will go your way, Jack, when you testify. Just use the excuse that you shot Wild Bill because he shot down your brother in Hays City."

"But I got no brothers," McCall says. "I only got sisters."

"Well, who the damn hell is gonna know that?" Black Jack riles back. "Whadda ya got, flyspeck for brains?"

The Avengers must laugh at McCall's stupidity as Kidd, Yellowstone, Gentles and Shannahan leave McCall's trial to deliver a companion to grace – Wild Bill's funeral preparation at Charlie Utter's campsite in White Wood Gulch.

Black Jack, Billy Kelly, O'Ryan and Johnston are staying with McCall's trial to make sure all goes well.

As Kidd's group of gangsters reach Utter's camp, they see that Colorado Charlie has company of his brother Steve and another character who goes by Charlie Storm.

This trio is the same three who are known about the Black Hills to trade horses to Indians and then kill the Indians during their sleep, so to steal the same horses. It is said that the Utter crew traded the same horses a dozen or so times.

The trio is now removing items from Wild Bill's wagon, as Kidd notices that Charlie Storm has one of Hickok's well known ivory-handled Colt revolvers tucked down in his belt.

"There's only one man who could handle those pistols fella," Kidd comments, "and you ain't him!"

"Yea," Storm rips, "well you ain't getting it 'cause I paid good gold for it. If you're a wantin' the other one, get it from Colorado."

"No thanks fella," Kidd says. "Ya wear a dead man's gun and you'll join 'im."

"Somebody's gotta pay for Hickok's box and plot," Charlie Utter cuts in. "Wild Bill was flat broke so I'm sellin' his stuff."

"Well, Utter," Yellowstone snaps in, "You earned it well enough."

Kidd glances at Wild Bill's body that the Utter crew has placed in an open casket and sees that Hickok's clothes have been changed to hide the knife wounds.

"Nice job, Charlie," Kidd says. "But what's this pile of hair here next to the casket? Whadya do, scalp 'im too?"

"Ah, it's just from the back of his head," Charlie Utter answers. "Who'll notice?"

"Gotta save sumpin' to give his wife," Charlie Storm smart mouths, "Jus' case she shows up."

"Well, Utter boys," Kidd says as he grabs the dead rabbit from Lance's spear, so to toss it into Wild Bill's open casket. "You can just replace Hickok's hair with this here HARE!"

As the quad of Irish depart Utter's camp to leave the trio of vultures to do their work on Wild Bill's carcass and belongings, Kidd comments to his buddies, "I can't place that Charlie Storm fella, but I know his voice from somewhere."

The four return to downtown to rejoin Jack McCall's trial, but it is already over and the four other Avengers of Black Jack, Billy Kelly, Tommy O'Ryan and John Johnston are found to be having a ball, drinking at the bar of the Number Ten Saloon with the judge and jury of McCall's trial.

It seems that the jury of miners love is for gold and not for Wild Bill.

Jack McCall has been found "not guilty" of the murder of Hickok, paid off by Black Jack Kelly, and sent on his way.

The Kellys are now thinking that Jack McCall is leaving Deadwood directly, going somewhere to start a new life and change his name to avoid being known as the one who back shot Wild Bill Hickok.

But no – A clown who finds his act in life will not leave the circus.

Colorado Charlie Utter Sitting In Grave

CHAPTER THIRTEEN
DON'T LET YOUR TONGUE CUT YOUR THROAT

In the afternoon of this August 3rd, many Deadwood residents pour out of the crannies, cracks and crevices of White Wood Gulch to pay respects at Wild Bill's funeral.

Besides the Utter brothers of Charlie and Steve, along with Charlie Storm to plant Hickok in the ground, other Black Hill notables are:

"White Eye" Anderson, with his one white eyebrow.

"Potato Creek" Johnny, who found an Idaho potato-sized gold nugget.

"Arapahoe Joe", a Caucasian-Indian half breed.

"Texas Jack", who came from Texas.

"Dunghouse Don", a prospector who spends more time hunkering in an outhouse than he does squatting along a creek bank panning his gold claim.

Now the female population of Deadwood is also well represented by characters fit for a carnival.

"Boss girl", Kitty Arnold and several of her Union Dance Hall Fairy Bellas.

"Canary Kate", an Irish girl related to the Kelly clan, who sits on a swing in an oversized birdcage at the dance hall, while chirping out songs.

"Wallboard Wanda", a Bella dancing girl with looks so sweet that a San Francisco artist has been painting a naked full portrait of her on the inside wall of an outhouse.

"Lollipop Lora", a White Wood street filly never seen without a candy stick in her mouth.

"Molasses Mae", the Asian-Black girl who worked her way to Deadwood from Ben Thompson's Bull Head Tavern in Abilene, Kansas.

And of course, Calamity Jane with her new partner, Hooligan Heidi and any other "Lonesome Dove" of Hells Half Acre.

Yea, it seems that in this year, 1876, about Deadwood, South Dakota, a person didn't fit in unless they had a nickname, a dub or a handle, to be a Deadwood Dude or Dude-a-Bell.

The sunset of August 3rd provides an atmosphere of jubilee about Deadwood. Jack McCall, now a free man, dressed in fine fancy duds, top hat to replace his old worn out sombrero, a new gold watch with chain and his pockets flush with money, is seen gallivanting throughout the finer gambling halls and saloons, in the clutches of the notorious fillies, Boss Girl, Kitty Arnold and Lollipop Lora.

McCall's jury of prospectors are excitedly celebrating, knowing that Custer's Avengers will soon be plunging and flushing hostile Indians out from hills, thusly providing for numerous fresh gold leads to safely explore.

Colorado Charlie Utter is ecstatic over reaping the rewards of auctioning off Wild Bill Hickok paraphernalia that includes locks of hair.

John Johnston is seen happily parading his fine Clydesdale horse up and down Main Street, with his belly full of livers as he blows Irish tunes out of his Scottish bagpipe. Sioux Indian heads dangle from his saddle, The Bella Union Dance Hall is holding its annual arm wrestling contest for the miners or any who dare to partake.

Black Jack "The Anvil" Kelly joins into the contest to take advantage of his years of duty as an Army blacksmith. He beats all takers with admiration from miners for the muscular forearm that bears the skull and sabers. Molasses Mae is on stage to tap dance and whistle, while handing Black Jack his trophy prize of a large gold nugget.

Canary Kate swings and sings as miners throw nuggets into her birdcage in hopes of persuading her to disrobe, so they can get a gander at her canary tattoo that she sports upon her buttocks.

The Number Ten features a tobacco-spitting contest. Even though it is considered a manly event, Calamity Jane is allowed to participate and put her best spit forward. As luck would have it, she out-spits all and walks off with the gold trimmed spittoon—a great accomplishment considering that she has been drowning her sorrow all day over the death of Wild Bill, with continuous shots of strong alcohol.

And men will cram the outhouse, where the artist is putting the final touches on the naked portrait of Wallboard Wanda, to view the masterpiece.

In several days following August 3rd, Jack McCall fails to heed the advice from the Kellys, to leave the Black Hills Territory for parts unknown and to start a new life. Instead, McCall loiters about Deadwood, where it doesn't take Boss Girl Kitty Arnold long to fleece him out of his short-lived wealth and gold watch to match. Kitty Arnold will hustle enough gold dust from the crooks and crannies of Deadwood and those who live in them, to plunk four thousand dollars down on a quarter-interest in the Cheyenne Lode and earn her new title from the local newspaper, "Quartz Queen of the Hills". How much of the down payment that had come from McCall's blood money will never be known.

Jack McCall returns to his true character of a broke, drunken town vagrant, with no place to go and no horse to get there. Being down and out, McCall makes the most blundering mistake of his useless life. A catatonic move that will carry him down the gutters of Deadwood and catapult him directly into the sewers of Hell.

McCall contacts Jack Kelly and "demands" more pay off or he could disclose to the newspapers the whole plot involved to get Wild Bill Hickok.

This threat only confirms Lance Gentles' statement that you can't trust a Limey. The Kellys now realize that Jack McCall will only be a continual problem and the fuse to his effacement must be lit. To get McCall out of Deadwood, so the Kellys can control his destiny without local suspicion, the Kellys promise to meet his demands.But McCall must leave town immediately and go to Laramie City, Wyoming to await the arrival of Black Jack Kelly with more payment. McCall, being broke, is given a horse and provisions by Kidd to make the journey. He has no weapon so Black Jack gives him the small caliber pistol that was used to mistakenly shoot card player Frank Massie. Jack McCall rides for Laramie City as the Kellys make plans to permanently silence him. McCall is *not* to be gunned down by the Irish gang, however. Instead, it must be made to look as if the U.S. Army is taking action to redeem the murder of an American hero, Wild Bill Hickok. This action would also chill any rumors that the Army and or its soldiers wanted Wild Bill dead.

McCall arrives in Laramie with no problem, where he waits for the Kellys to show up with more pay off. But instead of the Kellys showing up in Laramie to meet McCall, he is greeted by a patrol of other U.S. Army uniformed soldiers with a warrant to arrest him a second time for the murder of Wild Bill Hickok. Jack McCall is transported by the patrol back to South Dakota, but not to Deadwood, where he has already been found innocent. Instead, he is taken to Yankton, where the U.S. Army knows that they will be able to control the outcome of a second trial. Once McCall is safely in custody in Yankton, Black Jack Kelly visits him in his cell to tell him that there was some sort of mix up in Army orders and that if McCall could sit tight for a while, the Kellys would have time to get matters straightened out. But the Kelly clan returns to Fort Robinson, Nebraska, where another project is about to come their way.

CHAPTER FOURTEEN
DEN OF THE DEAD RABBITS

California Joe, who had backed Wild Bill's play that day in HaysCity, when soldier John Kelly was killed, had not been forgiven or forgotten by the Kelly clan. But before the Irish Avengers can cook up a course of action to extinguish him, Joe's stern dedication to avenge his departed partner vaults himself into the *Den of the Dead Rabbits*. Joe, who had been sent out of Deadwood by Charlie Utter the day that Hickok was killed, did not return to Deadwood until after Jack McCall had already left for LaramieCity. Joe will never learn the role that Charlie Utter played in the set-up of Wild Bill, but he figures that Jack McCall could not possibly have the guts to make a hit at Hickok by himself. McCall had to have had some strong backing for him to think he could back-shoot Wild Bill and not fear retaliation from any Hickok associates, while he lingered about Deadwood for several days. California Joe receives the answer he is looking for when a Deadwood resident informs him of the unknown men that were seen with Jack McCall, that wear the ghoulish tattoos upon their arms. This confirms to Joe that not all of the Irish Avengers and Dead Rabbits gangsters that lurked within the 7th Cavalry were killed at Little Big Horn. Joe, learning that Jack McCall has been rearrested, rides for Yankton to confront McCall in his cell. It doesn't take Joe long to squeeze the truth out of the squeamish McCall, and learn that there is no end to those damn Kelly's. Through asking about Yankton, Joe finds out that those who sport the peculiar tattoos headquarter at Fort Robinson, Nebraska.

California Joe rides for Nebraska, but decides to first stop off back in Deadwood to inform Hickok's good buddies of the true demise of their Pard. Joe has high hopes of recruiting them for vengeance. But California Joe is in for a rude awakening when he arrives at the Number Ten Saloon. To a man, and to one who dresses like a man, those who will later swear to being a good pal of the Prince of the Pistoleers steadfastly refuse to go with Joe and confront those who Joe feels are responsible for the murder of Wild Bill.

Arapahoe Joe squeals, "I wasn't stupid enough to go to Little Big Horn with Custer, Joe, nor foolish enough to come here to the Number Ten with Wild Bill. So I damn sure ain't dumb enough to go to hell with you, Joe, at Fort Robinson."

Calamity Jane serves up the prophetic quote of her life, "I wouldn't mind being buried next to Wild Bill some day, Joe, but not today!"

California Joe, becoming disgusted with those who claim to be great pals to Wild Bill, snaps at Charlie Utter, "What about you and your brother, Charlie? Hell, you boys are sportin' Wild Bill's pistols and gold watch!"

"Maybe so, Joe," Charlie Utter cuts back, "but I got 'em comin' and I'll be damned if I'm gonna be caught sportin' a dead rabbit."

California Joe barks back at the Utters, "Seems mightily curious that you sent me outta town so I couldn't cover Wild Bill's back. And I hear that you deserted him minutes before he was back-shot. We will see about Wild Bill's belongings when I return."

"You go to FortRobinson, Joe," White Eye Anderson cuts in, "and there be no return! Don't ya think we all weren't pissed that the bastard McCall was peacockin' around after Wild Bill was back-shot? But what was we a doin' with that damn gang a-backin' 'im?"

"Why, nobody knew they was in town till the shootin' was over. Then they come outta the woodwork like cockroaches from hell. Wearing shirtless vests showing off freaky tattoos up and down their arms."

"They sashayed into McCall's trial, armed to the gills, with two of 'em tossin' dead rabbits on the stage in front of the judge and jury, while they all hollered, 'Dead Rabbits Rule!' They were followed by some crazed-lookin' red bearded guy, wearin' a vest made of tree bark, while blowing a damn bagpipe."

"McCall's trial was a joke, Joe. I asked the judge if I should keep a record of McCall's trial.His words to that were, 'we don't need no lousy transcript.'"

"Why, the damn jury couldn't wait to get the trial over so they could get to the bar and drink that gang of crazy's free booze. Word now is, Joe, that the fool McCall let his mouth overload his ass, and them boys are fixin' to give 'im a quick ride to hell. Ain't none 'a us here itchin' to join Wild Bill in Boot Hill, Joe. Best leave it be."

California Joe offers no words to answer White Eye's statement, as he has just learned what the Kellys already know – that besides himself and Wild Bill, 'there ain't enough gunfighter guts in Deadwood to string sausage'.

California Joe barges out the front door of the Number Ten Saloon, for the last time, and departs from those he feels are 'The Deadwood Disgustables'. He rides alone for Fort Robinson, Nebraska, in hopes of redeeming his friend who had no others, Wild Bill Hickok. Joe has his faithful rifle, his trusted revolver, his steady long knife and his loyal mule named Maud, as his only backups.

But what Joe doesn't know is that by his stopping off in Deadwood for several days, he had allowed time for a soldier who had been guarding McCall in Yankton to get to Fort Robinson ahead of him and warn the Kellys of the coming attraction. When Joe rides up on Fort Robinson, the two usual U.S. Army sentries at the gate are absent. In their place, two dead rabbits swing from the entrance posts. Joe boldly ventures past the rabbit cadavers that signal as they did in New York City, *You are now entering into and on, the tundra of the Dead Rabbits*.

Joe does not bother to stop and read the crude notice painted on a piece of wood and tacked to a post.

All are welcome in, on, over,
Spend money at the bar,
While you're at it,
But if you've come to tread on us,
You'll be dancin' with a rabbit.

With no soldiers seen by Joe, he goes to the fort trading post, which also serves as a saloon. He inquires to the bartender and several civilians, to the whereabouts of the soldiers—asking, "Where are the bastards who wear the skull and sabers?" None in the saloon utter a note as Joe orders and downs several shots of cheap whiskey. Joe struts out of the trading post to confront some non-uniformed men that he sees standing in the yard. As he does so, one of the silent men in the post now comments, "The fox in the hare's den is now prey for the rabbit."

California Joe approaches the men in the yard and bellows a challenge for all to hear, "Any you backshootin' Kellys got the gall to face me?"

The three men in the yard run for cover as the answer to Joe's challenge comes from behind him, through the lips of an Army issue Remington .50 caliber carbine.

Just as had happened to his buddy Wild Bill, who had no trusted friend to cover his back, California Joe is shot from the rear. The powerful mountain man wavers back and forth like a tall pine in the winter wind, before timbering backwards into the dirt of Fort Robinson.

Kidd Kelly strolls out into the fort yard from his hidden position to confront the fallen California Joe, who is bleeding freely and breathing hard through a gap in his lung. Kidd kicks away the rifle that Joe still clutches in his hand.

Black Jack Kelly creeps out from his crevice with a smoking Remington in hand, as Yellowstone Kelly nonchalantly prances along.

Since it had been Kidd's bullet that took down Wild Bill Hickok, Black Jack was given the chance to redeem his "missed" shot that hit Frank Massie, by having the first crack at "backshootin" California Joe. After all, it's an Irish tradition to allow all clan members a piece of the vengeance.

Other soldiers now appear in the fort yard with four of them being the ones of the 14th Infantry who had gone to Deadwood with the Kellys – Billy Kelly, Lance Gentles, Snags Shannahan and Tommy O'Ryan.

The fort duty Army surgeon steps into the yard from his office. He is Dr. Valentine T. McGillycuddy. As the soldiers surround the dying mountain man, Kidd crouches down over Joe, to start in his pricking demeanor, "Got any sweet-smellin' tobacco, Joe? Like your buddy Hickok had on 'im

when we plucked 'im? I know you're hurtin', Joe, so don't bother a reachin'."

"I'll just help myself," Kidd jokes as he reaches into Joe's beaver pelt jacket to remove the tobacco pouch.

Kidd now straightens up to reach for his own smoking pipe and pack it with Joe's tobacco. Kidd tosses the pouch to Black Jack for a kill trophy, puffs on his lit pipe, and continues on in his pricking, "Now Joe, you should have kept to your buddy Wild Bill's rules for survival that day back in Hays City when you all had the drop on us Kellys. When you pull a pistol on a man, you had damn well better use it. You didn't, and I swore that someday when Hickok's back wasn't so well covered, I'd be there. I was and you wasn't. Now Joe, I got some bad news, but some good news for ya! Bad news – you're dead! Good news – you can now join your buddy Hickok in Hell!" Kidd growls the word "Hell", as he puts his cavalry boot to Joe's throat, to press down on Joe's adams apple and end the erratic breathing of a man that George Custer once called "half man, half horse, half alligator".

Dr. Valentine T. McGillycuddy, another fine Irish lad, true to his fellow countrymen and being of such indisputable integrity that some day a booze bottle of Schnapps will bear his name, reports in Army records that California Joe died from a gunshot wound inflicted by some deranged lunatic civilian who had it out for Joe. And with no other civilian law enforcement within hundreds of miles who is going to say otherwise?

But the U.S. Army is nice enough to see that poor Joe receives a fittin' funeral along the back of the White River that runs by Fort Robinson, for his years as a scout for George Custer. True to tradition, the Kellys add a little New York City Irish flavor to Joe's burial, by tossing in a dead rabbit for a relish.

This night, the Irishmen of Fort Robinson and any other soldiers wishing to join in revel along the bank of the river that runs by. They play Irish tunes on Cavalry instruments, to compliment an ole Irish custom from the homeland, of dancing a jig after a triumphant vendetta has been fulfilled. The jig is to be forever remembered as "The Irish White River Dance". John Johnston barbecues a large hindquarter of a four-legged animal for the festivities, as the four Kelly clansmen pass by.

Yellowstone Kelly cracks to the deep hollow eyed Scotsman, "What, no liver tonight, Johnston?"

"Na," the Master Avenger answers, "cuttin' down on the iron."

The liver eater smiles wide as Jack chows down on slab of cooked flesh.

"Got a sharp tang to it, Johnston," Black Jack belches. "What is it — elk?"

"Maud burger," the Scotsman answers, drawing sarcastic laughter from Kidd, Yellowstone and Billy Kelly.

"What the hell's so damn funny?" Black Jack yelps, as Kidd and Yellowstone amble off.

"You're eatin' California Joe's mule, Black Jack," Billy Kelly pops.

The Kelly clan had taken down two of the West's most deadly and feared gunmen – Wild Bill Hickok, the Prince of the Pistoleers, and California Joe, King of the Riflemen. Together, it would have taken a small army to take them out. But once each was separated from the other, with one unable to cover the other's rear, this deadly duo could be had. As the news of the killing of California Joe reaches the town of Deadwood, White Eye Anderson realizes that it was his last words to Joe, that christened Fort Robinson, Nebraska "The Fort of No Return".

"I tried to warn Joe," White Eye tells Calamity Jane. "If folks 'round here keep nosin' into the killin' of Wild Bill, that damn gang of freaks just might torch this town to the ground and turn Deadwood into charcoal."

At this time, White Eye Anderson does not realize his potential of being a wise prophet.

With the vengeance for the 7th Cavalry soldier, John Kelly, now complete, only one detail remains for the cover up—the shut up of the Deadwood Duffer, Jackleg McCall.

Dr. Valentine T. McGillycuddy

CHAPTER FIFTEEN
LIPS NOW SEALED

On December 5, 1876, Jack McCall goes to trial for the second time for the murder of Wild Bill. Even though McCall was already found innocent by a jury in the jurisdiction of the crime, there is no double jeopardy when it comes to General Phil Sheridan's Army. The Army arrests witnesses to insure that they appear at McCall's trial.

Before the trial starts, the Kellys tell McCall to stay calm. No matter the outcome, they will eventually get him cleared.

As in the first trial, no murder weapon is introduced and no two witnesses can corroborate the type of revolver McCall used. No one testifies to having actually seen McCall shoot Hickok, but only that they saw McCall standing over Wild Bill, after they heard a gun blast, and that McCall was trying to fire his pistol 5 or 6 times, but his gun wasn't firing. But it all doesn't matter because the Deadwood Duffer doesn't deny that he shot Wild Bill. This time he uses the excuse that he shot Hickok because Wild Bill had threatened to shoot him on sight.

McCall's lawyer puts up little defense on McCall's behalf, and does not insist that trying him a second time violates his constitutional right of no double jeopardy. But then as Charlie Utter put it, the lawyer, too, has no desire to be sportin' a dead rabbit.

Jack McCall is found guilty of the murder of Wild Bill and sentenced to be hung on March 1, 1877. Again, the Kellys tell McCall to just sit out the harsh winter in his warm cell, as they work on having the verdict overturned. Jack McCall sits out the winter of 1876-1877 in his jail cell in Yankton, South Dakota.

As it nears the time for his scheduled execution, McCall starts to get nervous. He again sends word to Black Jack Kelly, that he could talk to the newspapers if something is not done on his behalf. Black Jack visits McCall to calm him down. He falsely tells McCall that the President of the United States is going to issue McCall a pardon, because the shooting of Wild Bill Hickok took place in territory not yet part of the United States. McCall is to receive the Presidential pardon on the day of the scheduled hanging. The gullible Deadwood Duffer falls for the lie and the Kellys see to it that McCall is kept well supplied with fine whiskey as well as the drug opium to ease the pain of the wait. On occasion, a woman of leisure is sent by his cell.

Unknown to the Kellys at first, someone is making an attempt to get McCall's hanging stopped. Governor John Pennington signs a petition that will be sent to the President of the United States requesting that Jack McCall be given a full pardon. Pennington makes a statement to the press that he is opposed to the re-arrest of persons tried and acquitted in the Black Hills. His statement is written up in the "Deadwood Black Hills Pioneer News", on February 10, 1877, a little more than two weeks prior to March 1st.

Black Jack shows the newspaper to Kidd. "We might have a problem here, Uncle."

Kidd grabs the newspaper from Jack, so he can read the article for himself, as he enters into an outhouse. Within minutes a roar is heard to vibrate through the wood panels of the outhouse.

"What the hell is a Governor compared to the only god west of the Mississippi? This here paper will sure make for fine dung-wipe!" After getting done with his business, Kidd exits the outhouse with a stare at Black Jack. "There is NO President of the United States!" flares Kidd. "Why, that White House has seen more assholes than this here outhouse!"

(Because of charges of fraud in several states in the Presidential election of 1876 for the 1877 term that almost started a new civil war, there has to be a recount in votes and the results are not in as of yet. It had looked like Samuel J. Tilden had won the election over Rutherford Hayes.)

The petition for Jack McCall's pardon sits unopened on the desk of the Oval Office along with other documents that have to be signed by a President.

On March 1, 1877, Jack McCall is hung without a hitch of interference. McCall is so swollen from drug and alcohol abuse that the rope around his neck cannot be loosened after he is pronounced dead. The rope has to be cut a foot from the noose and Jack McCall is buried with the necktie that squeezed shut the tongue that cut his throat.

Several days later, Rutherford Hayes is sworn in as the 19th President of the United States. The Kelly joke is that Governor John Pennington's petition for Jack McCall's pardon "makes for fine White House dung-wipe".

CHAPTER SIXTEEN
IN THE SPIRIT OF LITTLE MARY

The ending of summer, 1877, makes it over one full year into the Custer Avenger's relentless pursuit of vengeance against the Sioux and Cheyenne Indians, to even the score for Little Big Horn. The Avengers take a temporary leave from the action in September, which allows the Kelly clan to hold a good ole-fashioned Irish hullabaloo at Fort Robinson, Nebraska. Besides the Kellys of Kidd, Yellowstone, Jack and Billy being on hand, boyhood pals Lance Gentles, Tommy O'Ryan and Snags Shannahan are also in attendance. Custer Avengers that include the Scotsman John Johnston are also in the audience.

For excitement, the Dead Rabbiteers are having a contest of throwing wooden spears at running Nebraska prairie rabbits that are let out of a box. Lance Gentles is taking his turn at demonstrating his knack of spear-chucking when an unexpected guest arrives on the scene.

Oglala Indian Sioux Chief, Crazy Horse, whom the U.S. Army has issued an arrest warrant for, surrenders himself to the Army brass of FortRobinson. He is the Indian on whom the Sioux Nation has bestowed the honor, "The Greatest of all Oglala Warriors". But, as California Joe had fatally learned one year ago, Fort Robinson, Nebraska, is no place to go if one (or one of its kind) had plod on the Kelly clan. And one of the Oglala kind HAD plod on little 5-year-old Mary Kelly.

The Dead Rabbiteers take full control of the surrender situation, when the Army brass of FortRobinson goes out for lunch. Once in custody, Crazy Horse is transferred by the Irishmen to a solitary blockhouse to get him away from the many other Indian eyes that loiter about the fort—a move that the Irish soldiers are hoping for. When the Oglala Chief sees that the blockhouse he is to be detained in has iron bars in the doorway and windows, he resists going in.

Lance Gentles, still in possession of his rabbit-killing wooden spear, drives the weapon into Crazy Horse's backside, causing the Chief to topple to the ground. Crazy Horse is now bleeding abundantly and is in pain. However, because many Indians begin to gather around the Chief, the Kelly's are unable to finish him off.

It doesn't help to calm the turmoil when John Johnston gargles out, "I'll give a dozen fine scalps for the Crazy's liver!"

The soldiers put on a masquerade that they are concerned for Crazy Horse's well being. They pick him up and carry him to the fort surgeon's office and place him on the operating table. And it just so happens that the good duty surgeon is the same fine Irishman who dotted the "i" on California Joe's death certificate, Dr. Valentine T. McGillycuddy. The doc stops the bleeding of the Oglala Chief and gives him opium to ease the pain. As matters calm down in the doctor's office, bystanders are ordered to leave so Crazy Horse may rest in his drug-induced delirium.

Billy Kelly and Snags Shannahan are put on guard duty to keep watch at the door to the surgeon's office. Late into the night, around midnight, Billy Kelly unlocks the rear door of the office, to let in his kin, Kidd, Yellowstone and Black Jack. Crazy Horse is now in the company of four unforgetting and unforgiving rabid Kelly clansmen seeking final retribution for little Mary. And one of these "Krazed Kellys" is carrying a bloody, live, kicking, long, thin jackrabbit!

The quad of Kelly's surround the army cot that the Oglala Chief rests on, with Yellowstone being at the head. Since Kidd and Black Jack had already knocked their men, Wild Bill and California Joe, out, it is only fair that Yellowstone be given the honor of carrying out this vendetta for the Kelly clan. Just as California Joe had, Crazy Horse will hear the last words spoken to him on earth, while lying on his back in the confines of The Fort of No Return.

Yellowstone with his large hands to match a grizzly's, wraps the bloody wounded rabbit around the Chief's neck while he looks down into the Indian's open, glassy, drugged eyes. "This is for little Mary Kelly, great Oglala Chief," Yellowstone growls. "You may not have been the Oglala who scalped Mary, but you wear the name, so you're in the game. Kelly's my name, avenging Mary my game! Take it to your Happy Hunting Grounds in the sky and may you be there a half-hour before the devil knows you're dead!"

Yellowstone tightens the rabbit that encircles the Chief's windpipe. He quickly twists the animal in a circular motion, to snap vertebrae of both the rabbit and the greatest Oglala warrior to ever live. The four Kelly's now all depart the Army surgeon's office, to go celebrate the clan's finest hour of retribution for little Mary and do another version of the Irish White River Dance.

Dr. Valentine T. McGillycuddy again, being loyal to his fellow countrymen, reports on record that Indian Chief Crazy Horse peaceably expired in his sleep. The good doctor just can't seem to explain how the jackrabbit died. But at least for a small conciliation, the great Oglala warrior did not die alone. U.S. Army records are made to indicate that Crazy Horse was lanced by soldier William Gentles' bayonet, because the U.S. Army has no classification for a New York City style rabbit-hunting spear.

General Phil Sheridan is highly pleased when he receives word that he could now toast to the riddance of the Sioux Indian Chief who had put his Army to shame at Little Big Horn.

CHAPTER SEVENTEEN
DODGE CITY DANDYS

In 1878, Kidd Kelly and nephew Black Jack figure it's time to fade out of U.S. Army life and let the Custer Avengers clean up on the Sioux and Cheyenne Indians. With the vendettas against Wild Bill Hickok, California Joe and Oglala Chief Crazy Horse carried out, the Kelly's had fulfilled their vows to their kin. Yes, the three Kellys who had been educated on the streets, alleys and parks of New York City, graduating from the University of Dead Rabbits, and obtaining degrees in gunology, had "knocked their man out". Kidd and Jack decide it is also the time to look in on ole Jim Dog Kelley. Jim Kelley had retired from the 7th Cavalry in time to keep from having to go to Little Big Horn with the Custer's. Kidd has heard that the Ole Dog has had the Luck of the Irish a second time, when he went to Dodge City, Kansas, to open that hunting dog breeding business he was itching for. Word is that Jim Kelley has hit it big and is running rampant on the streets of Dodge with a gang of his own.

But Yellowstone Kelly has ideas other than his kin, so he decides to hang out a while with the Custer Avengers. But if he becomes bored, Yellowstone will check in on Kidd and Black Jack in Dodge City.

Before going directly to Dodge City, Kidd desires to venture over to the Pine Ridge Indian Reservation, where he had left Willowee with her people some four years ago. Kidd had not found the time or chance to look in on her until his retirement from the U.S. Army. Kidd feels that the time may now be right to re-up with his ex-sidekick, Willowee, and take her on the trip to Dodge City. The U.S. Army assigns a small attachment of soldiers to escort the retired Kelly veterans of Kidd and Jack, to the Indian Reservation. Once the group of soldiers arrives at Pine Ridge, it doesn't take Kidd long to spot Willowee by her flowing long black hair. But she has changed otherwise. He sees that the beautiful Indian woman is pregnant with child. He learns from her that because she had not heard from him in a year since he had brought her here, she felt that he had no more need for a crippled Indian woman. Willowee then finally had agreed to marry a Lakota Sioux Indian brave who had longed for her to be his wife. Seeing that Willowee will now be having a family of her own, Kidd does not tell her that he has retired from Army life, for fear of her possibly wanting to run off with him and Black Jack.

Instead, Kidd tells Willowee, "I'll be a soldier boy till they bury me with my Cavalry boots on."

As Kidd, Black Jack and the Army patrol depart the Pine Ridge Reservation, Kidd ponders to himself the meaning of Willowee's last words to him, "I have had visions that once again I will lie in your powerful arms, looking up into your cougar eyes. But when that day does come, my tongue will no longer speak."

On to Dodge City, Kansas, where Kidd, along with his nephew Jack, does not have to venture far in his quest to locate ole 7th Cavalry buddy, Jim "Dog" Kelley. As they pull up their horses in front of the Alhambra Saloon, gambling hall and restaurant, they are confronted by three men, boldly strutting down the boardwalk, with a hound dog in tow. One of the three men looks as if he just stepped off a luxury boat from Ireland with his three-piece vested suit, derby hat to match, gold watch with chain, gold shamrock diamond-studded stickpin, and a fine walking stick which has an engraved gold handle. He is one decked-out leprechaun. The other two taller men are just as sharp in their threads of vested suits with top hats. These two are no doubt lawmen, wearing badges shining with reflected sunlight.

"I'll be damned!" shouts the leprechaun flanked by the lawmen. "Didn't think I'd see you two Kelly boys again until I got to hell! Figured you both caught it with the Custer crew."

"Hell no, you old hound dog," Kidd growls back. "Ain't no red devils quick enough to get us boys' livers."

Kidd and Black Jack dismount their horses, as Jim "Dog" Kelley introduces them to the two lawmen.

"These here are the Masterson brothers, Bat and Jim," Dog Kelley says. "What say we sashay into my saloon here for a few swigs and I'll fill you two Irish boys in on my deal here in Dodge City."

Once seated at the main round table of this saloon called the Alhambra, Jim Kelley informs Kidd and Black Jack of his prospering saloon and dog breeding businesses in Dodge. But Dog Kelley has had trouble with the law in Dodge, for his house and cribs of prostitution. The sheriff and city marshal wanted too big a cut. So to counter the situation, Dog Kelley formed a city gang of his own with the Masterson's and another set of brothers known as the Earp's. Jim Kelley ran for City Mayor and Bat Masterson went after the Ford County Sheriff position. Both were voted in by the fine citizens of the county. With Kelley and Bat now in charge, Wyatt Earp, Virgil Earp, Ed and Jim Masterson all became city or county lawmen. These six became what is known as the "Dodge City Gang". With the Dodge City Gang now in control there is no problem with running their drinking, gambling and prostitution enterprises about Dodge City.

Once Mayor Kelley finishes his story of the new situation about Dodge City, they are joined at the table by the rest of the Dodge Gang who has come for dinner. Wyatt Earp is with his Dodge City dove, Mattie and brother Virgil has his dollie, Allie. (Mayor Jim "Dog" Kelley has been cabareting about Dodge, arm in arm with the flamboyant theatre actress and singer, Dora Hand—so much so that the local newspaper has written them up as the Duke and Duchess of Dodge City.) A conversation starts as to what Kidd and Black Jack had been doing since Jim Kelley had last seen them, before the Little Big Horn battle. Mayor Kelley is pleased to hear the particulars of how the Kelly clan had reduced Wild Bill Hickok, California Jack, and Chief Crazy Horse to corpses, all doing time with rabbit cadavers.

These stories of vengeance impress the Masterson brothers, with Bat commenting, "I'm gonna make damn sure that in the future I check the arms of a man before I draw down on 'im. To make sure he ain't sportin' one of those freaky tattoos you Irish boys wear!"

This crack by Bat draws a laugh from all, as Dog Kelley requests menus from his restaurant that is joined to his Alhambra Saloon. "Dinner's on me, men," the Dog barks. "The special is liver and onions."

"Hell no!" Black Jack hoots. "I've seen enough bloody livers to last a lifetime!"

Uncle Kidd laughs and then tells the story of his and Jack's adventure with Absoroka Dapiek, John Johnston. The entire gang shakes their heads to the tally of the liver-eater as they all decide to pass on the special and order steak and spuds.

During dinner, Mayor Kelley invites Kidd and Black Jack to make Dodge City their home for a try with easy jobs to go along—only catch being that the two Kelly's would have to chisel off their buckskin attire and swagger about Dodge City in threads fit for New York City's Broadway.

Kidd and Jack take Jim Kelley up on his offer and the Mayor's gang has two more Dodge City Dandies. Bat Masterson takes a liking to their plug ugly derbies so he throws away his flat top hat for a round top derby. Of course, there are no leather or rag stuffings.

Many of the West's top gunmen will wander through Dodge City, giving it the dime novel tag, "The Kansas housing project for the West's most notorious gunmen."

With Mayor Jim Kelley at the helm, there is no end to the supply of entertainment at the opera house, gambling games, good liquor, rich food and of course, wild and woolly women. Hunting for antelope and other game on the plains of Kansas with Kelley's fast greyhounds is one form of relaxation for keeping the gun-eye sharp. The weekends hold horse racing events with Mayor Kelley and gambler, Bat Masterson, together booking all bets. Jim Kelley grows such a craving for the pony races that Kidd Kelly comments, "When Jim Kelley passes away, I'm gonna have his hyde formed into a woman's saddle, so the ole dog can lie in between the two things he's blown his money on! (women and horses)"

Mayor Kelley provides much Irish whoopla around Dodge City the summer and fall of 1878. But eventually the good city folk rehash their opinion of the Dog Kelley Gang, when times turn scandalous and bloody.

Dora Hand had jilted her previous lover, Jim "Spike" Kenedy, in order to run with the upper class Mayor Kelley. In a drunken row one night, Kenedy rides by Dog Kelley's house, firing his gun at the front master bedroom window and at the figure he sees sleeping in Kelley's bed. Kenedy flees Dodge City thinking he has killed the scoundrel who stole his love. However, Mayor Kelley had left town for several days and turned his spread and bed over to his Dodge City Darling, Dora Hand. Dora succumbs to the expiration date on the bullet meant for "The Dog". Spike Kenedy is tracked down by a Masterson-Earp posse. Bat Masterson stops Kenedy in his horses' tracks, with a rifle slug to his arm. Kenedy becomes despondent when the posse informs him that he mistakenly killed the woman he still loves. "Finish me off," is Kenedy's request to the posse. But the posse did not oblige and they return Kenedy to Dodge City for a hearing. Once back in Dodge, Kenedy's arm is seen to be irreparable from the damage caused by the .50 caliber bullet that tore flesh, muscle and bone asunder. Gangrene sets into his wound while he waits in jail for the law of Dodge to decide his fate. Hanging Spike Kenedy would be too quick a punishment, some say at his hearing, "Let the scoundrel suffer a slow death in his scourge and guilt at killing the woman he loved." Spike Kenedy's gangrene spreads as he is run out of Dodge City to parts unknown and the killing of the Dodge City Darlin' Dora Hand becomes Dodge City Kansas' most famous drive-by shooting.

Whereas Kidd Kelly fares well about Dodge City by keeping with the company within the Dog's gang, nephew Black Jack's actions cast a much darker shadow. Jack Kelly has been lurking about the city in the company of a man that William "Billy the Kid" Bonney will later describe as a "colder, bloodier killer than myself". This gunman who Jack Kelly befriends is known among the gunmen as "The Deranged Dave Rudabaugh". Bat Masterson wises Kidd of Dave Rudabaugh's traits. "He's a cattle rustlin' crazed killer that would cut your throat in your sleep all for the price of a cheap whore! He's a buddy back stabber who turned on his partners after a blocked train robbery. Rudabaugh turned state's evidence and went scot-free while his buddies went to Leavenworth Prison. I wouldn't want to be anywhere near 'im when those boys get out."

Kidd in turn warns his nephew that Rudabaugh is "bad medicine" and teaming with 'im will lead to doing time in prison or much longer in Boot Hill. However, before Black Jack can decide what direction to go concerning Dave Rudabaugh, some other character shows up in Dodge City to make that decision for him...at least for a little while.

Dodge City Mayor, Jim 'Dog' Kelley

Courtesy Kansas State Historical Society

Dodge City Gang

Seated Left to Right: Charles Bassett, Wyatt Earp,
    M.C. Clark, Neil Brown.

Standing Left to Right: W.H. Harris, Luke Short,
    Bat Masterson.

Courtesy Kansas State Historical Society

CHAPTER EIGHTEEN
A STORM BEGINS TO BLOW

Early in 1879, a horse drawn stagecoach arrives in Dodge City on its usual run. The stage pulls up to a halt in front of Dog Kelley's, Alhambra Saloon, as the two Kelly's of Kidd and Jack are having lunch in a booth. A large figure of a man totally wrapped in buckskin attire steps out through the coach's door. Once the only stagecoach traveler receives his luggage from the driver, he struts into the Alhambra while shaking the spring's light snowfall from himself. He walks to the bar and asks the bartender if he knows anyone who sports a tattoo the likes of the one that he displays on his forearm, that of a skull and sabers. Before the bartender can answer, Kidd and Black Jack immediately recognize the man's rough voice as being that of their kin, Yellowstone Kelly.

After the usual "good to see ya" and "how ya been doin'?" Yellowstone informs his kin the reason of his arrival in Dodge City. He has come to deliver an important message of a possible threat to the Kelly clan. It seems that Charlie Storm, the sidekick of the Utter brothers about Deadwood, has been attempting to sell to any publisher who will listen, the real story behind the assassination of Wild Bill Hickok. Not knowing how many characters may now be in the Utter gang, Yellowstone figures he might not be able to go it alone in permanently shutting up this Charlie Storm. Kidd's answer to Yellowstone is, "We don't need another Hays, Kansas. We will all handle this Deadwood Charlie Storm situation and we'll stop off at FortRobinson to see who-all wants to come along."

The three Kelly's of Kidd, Yellowstone and Black Jack, waste no time in preparing for their trip to Deadwood, and after informing Dog Kelley of their departing for a while, they ride for Fort Robinson, Nebraska.

On arrival at the fort, the three Kellys are greeted by soldiers Billy Kelly, Tommy O'Ryan and Snags Shannahan. They are given the bad news that senior Dead Rabbit's Lance Gentles had passed away in 1878.

Billy, Tommy and Snags get leave from their duties and the seven Irish thugs who had ridden to Deadwood in '76 are now six, to return for "Operation Mop-Up".

On this return trip to Deadwood, in 1879, the six Irish Avengers split into three's to search and plunge the saloons, gambling halls, prostitution cribs, Chinese opium dens and White Wood Gulch, where Charlie Storm and the Utter brothers had once camped near Wild Bill Hickok in the summer of '76.But neither Storm, nor the Utter brothers are anywhere to be found.

Deadwood citizens are cold to the Irish gang's questions, making it seem that they may be in fact, harboring Charlie Storm from view.

It's a cold, windy fall night in the Black Hills of Dakota, as the six Irish Avengers gather to drink around a table in a curtain-closed booth of the BellaUnionDance Hall, to discuss the Charlie Storm situation.

All six agree that it is time to move on, with the residents of town making it impossible for them to accomplish their task.But "tasks" can be altered, and the six all desire some sort of satisfaction, for their journey not to be a totally wasted operation.

Billy Kelly brings up a suggestion as he looks across the table at Kidd. "Ya know, a lad would have a hard time trying to explain a Charlie Storm theory that soldiers were involved in the killin' of Hickok, if the last bit of real evidence were to be eliminated."

"And just what might that be?" Kidd responds.

"The murder scene of the Number Ten Saloon and the archway to the Bella Union that you and Jack shot through," Billy answers.

"And that's what I'm here for," Pyro Tommy O'Ryan cuts in. "I'm never without the tools of my trade. This here town of Deadwood and its smart-ass citizens will think General Sherman went through here on his march to the sea, when I toss 'em a few Tommybombs."

Yellowstone Kelly cuts in with his bit of suggestion. "The bakery shop. It's got ovens going all night that hold as much wood as a locomotive. If they were to get outta hand in this night's wind, nobody'll stop 'er."

"That be it, Tommy," Kidd continues. "You'll just have to go bake yourself a loaf of black powder and turpentine bread tonight."

"Yea," Snags Shannahan adds. "And like we use ta say on Broadway, it'll be the toast of the town."

The gang laughs in unison as Black Jack, wanting to get into the conversation with his bit of humor, remarks, "And it just might smoke up one hell of a Storm."

Into the darkness of night, the six Irish thugs accomplish their dastardly deed, with the aid of O'Ryan's Tommybombs. The entire block of Deadwood that houses the Number Ten Saloon, Bella Union, Crumbs of Comfort and other buildings on Main Street will be obliterated.

The six ride out before the next day's sunrise, with the blazing town of Deadwood to light their way. Pyro Tommy requests that they stop on the ridge overlooking the town, so to get one last look at his climatic achievement of destruction. As they do so, Kidd gives his final thanks to his boyhood buddies who had ridden to Deadwood for this second time. This Dead Rabbit adventure is the final time that these six Irish gangsters will ever get together. Yellowstone Kelly is returning to Fort Robinson with soldiers Billy Kelly, O'Ryan and Shannahan. Kidd and Black Jack are going back to Dodge City and they're taking along Canary Kate Kelly. She has had her fill of Deadwood and what's she to do now that her kin has turned Deadwood to charcoal and melted away her birdcage.

Deadwood's "mysterious" fire of 1879

CHAPTER NINETEEN
A DOG PACK SPLITS

Times aren't the same about Dodge City when Kidd and Black Jack return. The Dodge City Gang is losing its grip on the city. As all gang life goes with its criminal and immoral activities, the respectable majority of the county will become fed up and the Dog Kelley Dodge City Gang is no exception. The downslide in Kelley's popularity had all started with the needless drive by shooting death of the very popular entertainer, Dora Hand. Although it had been Spike Kenedy who had shot and killed Dora, many residents felt that it was Mayor Kelley's womanizing that led to her demise. Dora Hand was not the only woman belonging to another man who was stolen by "The Dog". Yeah, you might say that Kelley was just living up to his nickname.

Bat Masterson's popularity took a dive when he deserted his sheriff duties to join Ben Thompson in doing some highly paid work for the railroad near the Colorado/New Mexico border. There was much speculation about Bat and Ben's "double dealin" the railroad companies that were fighting for the rail rights. Bat Masterson not only lost his backing in Ford County, Kansas while he was away, but he lost his brother, lawman Ed Masterson in a gunfight with several cattlemen in Dodge. Bat wasn't there to back his brother Ed's play, just as California Joe had taken a ride rendering him unable to cover Wild Bill Hickok.

An anti-gang movement called the *Reformers* had risen in Dodge City in 1879, going against Mayor Kelley and Sheriff Bat Masterson. Jim Kelley and Bat Masterson along with their cronies will all be out of office in the next elections. The Earp brothers were leaving Kansas with their 'White Doves' heading for Las Vegas, New Mexico. They are taking along a new member of the Earp Gang, a dentist turned gambler and gunfighter, Doc Holliday. Alongside Doc is his dive-bomber, Big Nose Kate. After all, the boys have got to have the girls along for protection—protection from the elements of not having enough cash for room, board and, of course, gambling with drink. There will be no welfare or food stamps available in Las Vegas. It's said about the West that if pimps desire to go to a place called Las Vegas, they had better bring along some Dollies to hustle up some cash.

The Kellys of Kidd, Jack and Kate realize that the party in Dodge City is about to hear "the fat lady sing", so the three decide to go take a peek at this place called Las Vegas. The trio of Kellys is several hundred yards from the town limits of Las Vegas when they notice a peculiar looking tall structure sitting in the middle of town. It resembles a crudely built large wooden windmill. Some type of object is hanging from one of the mill's blades. The Kellys cautiously approach the center of town with their weapons ready. They soon identify the strange hanging object. It is a large black dog swinging in the wind. Circling the windmill in the town plaza are dancing and singing children.

Kidd, remembering back to his days of youth in New York City when his gang had hung dead rabbits, comments to Jack and Kate, "Looks like we just wandered into the den of the Dead Dog Gang."

Black Jack looks at the children and states, "I'm just glad this bunch of hooligans is still too young to be armed."

"Don't bet on it, Jack," Kate adds.

The Kellys decide to stop and have a drink at any saloon that has a good route of escape. They have no idea of what may lie ahead. They locate one that has only one customer along with the bartender. Once in the saloon, Kidd eases up as he sees that the customer at the bar is one who had been a lawman for a while with the Dodge City Gang. He is the "mysterious" Dave Mather. Dave had gotten his nickname from mysteriously showing up or leaving without so much as a peep. Where Dave Mather had come from nobody knows. This mysterious Dave greets the three with, "Is there anywhere I can go without runnin' into one of you Kelly's?"

The three Kellys look puzzled as to the meaning of Dave's statement until the bartender cuts in, "Welcome, I'm Ed 'Kelly' of Missouri way."

Kidd, Jack and Kate learn from this bartender named Kelly, that he is kin to Josiah Kelly, the husband of Fanny Wiggins. They also find out from Dave Mather and Ed Kelly that the Earp Gang was here in Las Vegas but had recently left for Tombstone, Arizona. Mather continues his story by saying The Earp's nor Doc Holliday could handle the tension about Las Vegas with it being run by a character named, "Hoodoo Brown" and his lawmen, Dave Rudabaugh and John Webb.

Doc Holliday attempted to settle down in Las Vegas with Big Nose Kate, by opening up a dental clinic. But Holliday couldn't control his drinking and gambling habits and lost all his holdings in a high stakes poker game to someone he later claimed was a 'high heeled card shark'.

Her name was Lottie Deno. Named from the Spanish phrase, "Lotta Dinero" (lots of money).

Holliday had broke her man in the poker game so she stepped in to clean the Doc out. She finished him off with her last poker hand of three queens, spades, diamonds and clubs. Doc Holliday had bet it all on his three jacks.

HooDoo Brown, who likes giving out nicknames to those that he thinks earned them, stated, "Doc Holliday was busted outta Las Vegas by four queens." Lottie Deno was the 4th and the "Gambling Queen of Hearts".

But before Holliday left town with the Earps, he attempted to pull a con game that almost got him hung out to dry at the town windmill.

Doc bet some of the town elderly and feeble that he could throw three dice and make the tops and bottoms add up to twenty-one. Holliday collected on a few bets until HooDoo Brown showed up at the Old Senior Home and demonstrated to the victims that three dice always come up 21, tops and bottoms.

Poor Doc, he had to pull out all of his sweet heart Big Noses Kate's gold teeth caps to clear his bad bets and skip out of town.

"What Doc Holliday and Big Nose Kate had brought to Las Vegas, stayed in Las Vegas".

Dave Mather ends the tale as Kate Kelly inquires, "What's with the hung dog in the town plaza?"

"Vigilantees," Dave states. "They pulled some guys outta jail in the dead a night and hung 'em at the windmill. They were still there swingin' in the wind when those young scalawags saw 'em on their way to school next mornin'. So now the youngin's round here are hangin' local pets. Town council figures on tearin' down that old windmill before those little rascals run outta animals and start on their parents."

After hearing the layout of the doings about Las Vegas from mysterious Dave, Kidd decides to leave for a friendlier climate. "I got no intentions of hangin' out in a town run by some guy who goes by 'Hoodoo', or playing poker with a local witch who's named after a Lotta Dinero and it sure is a mystery as to why you're still here, Dave."

Kidd and Canary Kate are moving on to Prescott, Arizona, whereas Black Jack has other ideas. He decides to hang out in Las Vegas a while with Ed Kelly—and the two are talking about goin' on south to Lincoln County, New Mexico. Word out from there is that they're paying good money for gunmen for the county war. They will eventually come in contact with a chap called "Billy the Kid".

When Kidd and Kate reach Prescott, they head down Whiskey Row to get coffee and breakfast at a saloon named the Birdcage—just Kate's kind of place. The owner of the Birdcage takes a liking to Kate Kelly and offers her a job as a bartendress. Before long, the saloon owner cuts a large hole in the ceiling of the place to lead up to the second floor. He builds a large birdcage, big enough to hold a human and able to be lowered down through the hole and into the saloon. Canary Kate Kelly "rides again" in the Birdcage Saloon, Whiskey Row, Prescott, Arizona. Now that Kate is all set with employment and a place to stay, Kidd Kelly rides on to Tombstone, Arizona.

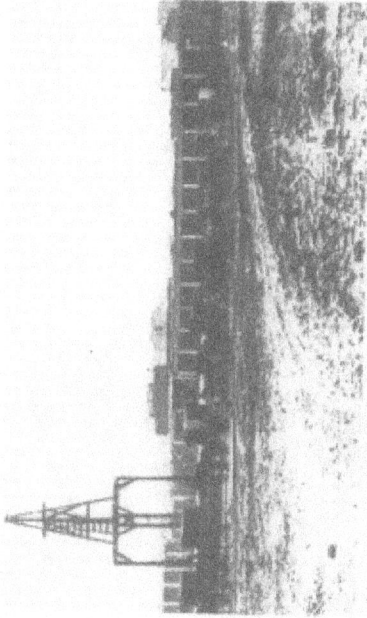

Hanging Windmill, Las Vegas NM

John 'DOC' Holliday
Courtesy Kansas State Historical Society

Mysterious Dave Mather

Courtesy Kansas State Historical Society

Billy the Kid

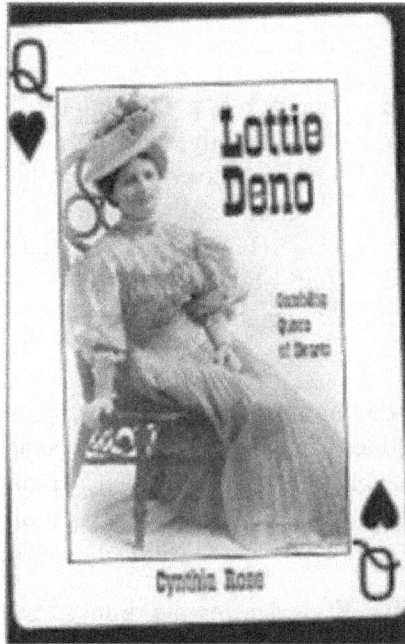

Q ♥ Lottie Deno

Gambling Queen of Draw

Cynthia Rose

CHAPTER TWENTY
ROAD KILL

By the year 1883, Tombstone, Arizona became the new residence for ex-citizens and or fugitives of Dodge City, Kansas. They have come to get in on the action of the latest metal mining boomtown. The city was named for the man who discovered the silver that caused the rush. He had been told that the only thing he was going to find in these here mountains would be his tombstone. He found silver. The Earp brothers of Wyatt, Virgil and Morgan are town lot owners, silver claim investors and city marshals. The Earps are having a running feud with the county sheriff and a clan known as the Clanton's. Doc Holliday lurks on the side of the Earp's. A character named Luke Short, who had been with Jim "Dog" Kelley's gang in Dodge City for a while, operates a saloon called the Oriental. Molasses Mae is in charge of his troupe of oriental girls.

It is a crisp winter day in the month of February, when Kidd is enjoying a beer at the bar of the Oriental with Bat Masterson, as Luke Short tends bar. The three are having a sociable chat when a drunken man storms in the front door demanding whiskey. Short, telling right off that the man is well intoxicated, refuses him with, "You've already had enough, fella."

Kidd Kelly immediately recognizes the drunk. "Well, if it ain't Charlie Storm, and I see that you're still sportin' Wild Bill's pistol," referring to an ivory-handled Colt revolver in a holster on Storm's belt.

Luke Short, who is well aware that Hickok was known to carry two ivory-handled Colts, but does not know that Storm may only have gotten one, comments, "Whadya do, fella, hock Wild Bill's other one for a bottle?"

The drunken Charlie Storm, knowing who Luke Short must be, flares back, "I only need one gun and one bullet to kill you, Short Shit!"

It is the wrong remark to make to the 5 foot 5 inch Luke, who is sensitive about his height. Luke hurdles from his position behind the bar, to face off with Storm.

Bat Masterson, the peacemaker, steps in between the two and gets in a crack of his own. "It's best ya haul ass outta Tombstone, Mister Storm, before you're put under one." Bat, gently putting his hand on Storm's shoulder, walks him towards the front door before matters turn deadly.

However, Kidd Kelly, who has said nothing thus far, knows that matters must somehow turn deadly for this Charlie Storm. For it is Storm who had made the threat to disclose that a gang of U.S. Army soldiers had been behind the murder of Wild Bill Hickok. Masterson walks Storm out the front door of the saloon and across the street to the hotel, where Bat advises him to sleep off his drunk.

As Bat does so, Kidd comments to Luke Short as the two of them look out the window of the saloon to keep watch. "That Storm needs a-killin'."

"AndI'll be a-doin' it," Luke answers back.

Bat Masterson returns to the Oriental Saloon to continue his drinking with Kidd and Luke. But, as some storms do, the one that had blown through the Oriental this day, attempts a return engagement within the hour. Charlie Storm fails to sleep it off and staggers out from the hotel to stand in the middle of the street out front of the Oriental, so to blow out a challenge. "Show your face, Short Shit, and stand before the new *Prince of the Pistoleers.*"

Luke Short, with his blood now at a boil, vaults over the saloon bar a second time, to plow out the front door, with no hitch in his gait. Masterson, wisely knowing not to interfere this time, has snappily stepped aside. Kidd Kelly's memory has been jolted by Storm's hillbilly-accented comment, "Prince of the Pistoleers". Kidd now recalls that Charlie Storm is the same third man who had ridden out of Hays City with Wild Bill Hickok and California Joe, that day years ago when John Kelly was shot down. "Now there's two reasons to kill him," Kidd says to himself. Kidd draws his Colt .45 and darts out the saloon rear door.

Short is already off the boardwalk out front and in a gallop towards Storm, who still stands in the street. Charlie Storm sees Short approaching, so he reaches for his ivory-handled Hickok souvenir pistol. But there will be no more magic in the pistol of Wild Bill. Storm displays a wide-eyed expression as a .45 caliber slug rips into his back. Kidd, who was not taking the chance that the vermin Storm might win or survive this confrontation with Luke Short, had fired his revolver from his position in the alley alongside the Oriental. Storm sways while holding his stomach wound, from where the .45 slug exited. Luke Short, now in Storm's face, presses the barrel of a pistol into Charlie's chest. Luke squeezes the trigger, blasting and dissecting Storm's heart, to finish him off.

Charlie Storm, who, like Jack McCall, had let his tongue cut his throat, now becomes Tombstone road kill and will go on to be a permanent tenant with the senior citizen's, of the Boot Hill housing project. Yes, Storm had come to Tombstone to find his tombstone.

Where Wild Bill Hickok's ivory-handled revolver goes after it made its appearance on the street of Tombstone, Arizona, is anyone's guess. Neither Kidd Kelly, Luke Short, nor Bat Masterson care little to "Wear a dead man's gun and you'll join 'im."

As good friends do, Luke Short takes full credit for the kill of Charlie Storm and the fine law enforcement of the town of Tombstone, the Earps, rule the shooting self-defense.

Within the next month, a stagecoach is held up by outlaws. The coach driver and a passenger are killed by the robbers. When Doc Holliday's female companion, Big Nose Kate, is beat up by the Doc, she squeals. She makes a statement to the local judge saying Holliday was behind the holdup. Holliday escapes prosecution when the Earps give up an alibi for the Doc. They also claim that Kate was highly intoxicated when she gave the statement. Kate hides out and some say she got her nickname Big Nose from sticking her nose into the Earp Gang's business. But Kidd Kelly knows otherwise. Kate wasn't born with a big nose but when Doc Holliday used her face for a punching bag, her nose was continually being broken and flattened by the Doc. One of the laws of the West is that "a whore sticks by her pimp". However, Kate has finally had enough and Doc Holliday will not see her big nose again until it leers at him on his deathbed.

It's a nice warm day in the desert town of Tombstone in 1881, when a large horse drawn wagon the likes of a prisoner van pulls up to a stop in front of the Oriental Saloon. The wagon is greeted by Molasses Mae, who is starting her day by tap dancing on the saloon's boardwalk. She is curious to why the wagon is not holding any law breakers. Instead, in this large caged wagon, sits a huge brown bear. A man dressed up like a circus pitchman sits upon the driver seat. This man steps down off the wagon to enter into the crowded Oriental, to speak his piece. Mae follows along without missing a step in her tap. The pitchman tells the saloon crowd that he has come to Tombstone to offer any cattle rancher in the area, a "sporting event of high stakes".

"And just what might that be?" Bartender Luke Short questions.

"My bear against any's bull in a fight to the death," the stranger answers.

Bat Masterson, in attendance, steps in front of the man to state, "What's the purse?"

"Winner gets half the gate money and a five hundred dollar side bet with me," the stranger says.

Wyatt Earp, who just happens to own a small herd of Texas Longhorns, now gets into the conversation. "Make it five hundred in gold and you got your challenge," Wyatt remarks.

The pitchman and Wyatt shake hands on the deal and one thousand in gold is put into the Oriental's iron safe as the crowd bears witness.

The beastly confrontation is to be held at the Tombstone cattle fairgrounds. The day of the match draws a large crowd with youngsters climbing telegraph poles to get a good view. Local town bankers are booking and holding all bets. Wyatt's prize longhorn steer proudly struts in the center of the fairground's arena while displaying his massive set of over 3-foot horns. The crowd gasps as the pitchman lets out his giant sized brown bear from the wagon. It's a "grizzly". The bull doesn't hesitate to charge. Putting his head down and driving it up at the standing bear when he meets him, for the kill. But the grizzly is an old hand at fighting bulls and has the moves of a matador. On the bull's third charge, the giant bear pounces down on the bull's back, "grabbing the bull by the horns". The bull feverously bucks in attempt to throw the grizzly, who is sinking his razor sharp fangs into the bull's neck in hopes that he will break vertebrae. But before the bear can complete the kill, the bull stumbles forward in a summer-salt, landing the bear on its back and the weight of the massive bull on top. The flip knocks the wind out of the grizzly, but the powerful bear has ripped off one of the bull's horns. The bull gets to his feet first and when the bear rises up, the bull is ready with his one last horn. The longhorn drives his head up into the grizzly's midsection to impale him. Both beasts now locked together by a horn, collapse as one into the blood soaked dirt of the corral. The crowd waits to see which beast will arise first to claim victory, but the wait goes on. Both animals breathe hard and bleed fast.

A woman in the crowd is heard to shout, "Shoot 'em to put 'em out of their misery!"

Wyatt Earp shouts louder, "I'll shoot the first one that touches 'em. I got good money on this and we all will be a waitin' it out!"

The wait goes to sundown with only the by-standers left that had made a wager. The grizzly breathes his last first, making the bull the declared winner.

The Earp Gang is jubilant as Wyatt declares, "It 'ill be bull and bear steak at the Oriental for all!"

Because the bull charges with his head down then brings it up for the kill, and the bear pouches downward to make his attack; it becomes the custom of the local mining stock investors to use the terms, "if stocks go up on price, it's a bull market, if stocks go down it's a bear market". These terms spread around the country all the way to New York City's Wall Street. And it's all because of this bull-bear fight in Tombstone, Arizona.

But the bull-bear duel is not the only confrontation held within a corral of Tombstone this year of 1881.

A feud has been going on between the Earp-Holliday gangs and a crew run by Ike Clanton. Bat Masterson and Luke Short, though both friends of the Earps, want no piece of this action. Masterson and Short leave Tombstone in time to miss out of the fun that transpires at the shootout of the OK Corral in October.

Kidd Kelly keeps to being just a spectator and spends his warm Tombstone winter days drinking in the Oriental Saloon. Molasses Mae drives him crazy with her tap dancing and whistling.

CHAPTER TWENTY ONE
CUSTER'S GOLD

The last day of this year 1881, New Year's Eve, Kidd Kelly is attempting to drink away his boredom at a rear table of the Oriental Saloon, Tombstone, Arizona. He has an itch to move on, but is wondering to himself a question that has remained unanswered since last summer.

In the month of last August, Kidd had heard word that the outlaw Billy the Kid had been shot and killed by a Sheriff Pat Garrett, in the month of July. Kidd knew from letters that he had received from Black Jack, that Billy the Kid had made the acquaintance of Jack and Ed Kelly. However, Kidd has not received any mail since the killing of the Kid, causing concern for the well-being and whereabouts of his nephew Jack.

Just minutes before the stroke of midnight and the New Year 1882, the answer to the question that Kidd has been pondering, sashays through the front door of the Oriental Saloon.

The answer is a ragged and dusty-looking man, who looks as if he rode in sitting on the front end of a locomotive, out of control. But nevertheless, he is easily recognized by Kidd, as his kin, Black Jack Kelly—and does nephew Jack have a tale to tell his uncle!

Just within the last month of December, Black Jack, Dave Rudabaugh and John Webb broke out of the Las Vegas, New Mexico, jail. While staying in Las Vegas, Jack Kelly made the dangerous mistake of hooking up with the "outlaws turned lawmen turned outlaws", the Deranged Dave Rudabaugh and John Webb. Jack had gone along with the pair on some type of bank heist. Jack does not inform Uncle Kidd of all the details and Kidd, being satisfied to just seeing his nephew still alive, only states, "I knew if you stayed in a place named Las Vegas too long you'd eventually have the Hoodoo put on your ass!"

Black Jack continues his story by saying that once he was clear from the law, he and Ed Kelly came to the conclusion that if they kept teaming up with Dave Rudabaugh, they would wind up balleting at the end of rope. Seeing the light, the two Kelly's high-tailed it out of New Mexico in separate directions. Ed Kelly was going back to his home state of Missouri, in an attempt to hook up with his kin, the Younger brothers. Jack refused

Ed's offer to go along and instead came to Tombstone to locate Kidd. (And Dave Rudabaugh would eventually go on to the country of Mexico, where the people there will greet him by lancing off his deranged head.)

With Black Jack now reunited with his uncle, Kidd suggests a new and exciting adventure.For the last near eight years since George Custer's 7ᵗʰ Cavalry had discovered gold in the Black Hills, Dakota Territory, Kidd has been secretly holding maps to the original find. Custer was not dumb enough to report to the government the richest gold leads. His intentions were to have his 7ᵗʰ work the mother lode at a later date. But Little Big Horn blew a hole in George Custer's mining plans. Kidd, with the only known existing map, feels the time is now ripe to pick the fruit.

Black Jack fully agrees with his uncle and these two Kellys dump horse manure on the road out of Tombstone, Arizona.

Winter is winding down in the Black Hills when Kidd and Jack reach Deadwood. They discover that some new furniture has been added on Main Street, since the fire of 1879. The saloons and gambling halls have all been resurrected—but The Number Ten Saloon and the Bella Union Dance Hall are not side-by-side, as in the past.

Now, the buildings in Deadwood are not the only things that have changed since the Kelly's were here last there in '79. The mountain terrain has been altered due to near ten years of weathering. Rains, snow, icing and thawing have carved new creeks and swallowed some old ones.

Kidd and Jack are searching in a remote area for the 7ᵗʰ Cavalry's original gold discovery when they come upon an old run-down miner's shack that looks abandoned. They enter in to find a frozen corpse of a miner, with his arms wrapped around a one-inch thick by twelve-inch wide, six-foot plank of wood. After closer examination, the Kelly's recognize the corpse as being the miner called "Dunghouse Don". Don's arms are wrapped around the outhouse plank that bares the portrait of Wallboard Wanda. Don's lips are frozen stuck to Wanda's wooden ones.

But Don's corpse is not the only thing that Kidd discovers. Don had built the shack up against a rock ledge. It's the ledge that Custer's men had marked by chiseling out the number seven, to mark the find of the Custer Gold.

The Kellys transport Don's body to town and the Kellys foot the bill to give ol' Don a fittin' funeral. After all, Don kept a good guard over the

Custer treasure. Wooden Wanda accompanies Don in his coffin but only after the boys about Deadwood make it legal with a good old Irish whiskey wedding.

Once settled in to a campsite, the two Kellys use the spring, summer and fall to work the creeks and gullies of the Black Hills to find that gold that is foretold by the Custer map. The work is hard, but it pays off well beyond the Kelly's dreams. Once the snow of winter starts to set into the hills, they trade their horde of gold nuggets for U.S. notes backed by gold or silver.

The two Kellys of Kidd and Black Jack, who have spent the last many years on the plains and mountains of the Western Frontier, decide as one mind that it is now the right time to return east and give a visit to the kinfolk and boyhood buddies of New York City—especially now, with their purses flush with a "lotto dinero".

CHAPTER TWENTY TWO
THE MORGUE

The year 1883 sees the Kidd and Black Jack arrive by train into New York City to carry out their wishes of visiting their old stomping grounds.

The first few days in the city are spent looking up other members of the Kelly clan. Kidd houses with his sister Kolleen, whereas Black Jack chooses to live upper class, in one of Manhattan's finer hotels. It doesn't take long for these two Kelly Army veterans to locate their ole Irish pals of the Lower East Side.

These fellow Dead Rabbits pals now all belong to the over 500 member, all Irish gang, the dreaded WHYOS. The WHYOS have been terrorizing and controlling the Fourth Ward of the city since the end of the Civil War. The vicious WHYOS gangsters and hit men headquarter at the Mulberry Bend, with the Irishmen doing their drinking and socializing at a saloon rightly named The Morgue.

Kidd and Jack are invited to join their fellow Dead Rabbits at The Morgue, by Kolleen Kelly's boyfriend, Danny-Boy. Danny-Boy is one of several WHYOS gang captains, with his charge being prostitution rackets. Kidd initially frowns on his sister's gallivanting and cabareting about the city in the limelight with the notorious Danny-Boy, but he says not a word of discouragement. After all, this is the sister and Kelly girl who has held the young Kelly clan afloat in those days of poverty just before the U.S. Civil War. The Irish respect the wishes of those who sacrifice to keep their clan together.

Some of the WHYOS gangsters of The Morgue are at first cold to the two "western" Kellys who Danny-Boy introduces to them. But the WHYOS Irish pride comes to the front when they hear that it is fellow New York City Dead Rabbits that caused the obliteration of western big shots Wild Bill Hickok, California Joe and Sioux Indian Chief Crazy Horse. For they, too, had read western dime novels.

Once the Kellys' stories are told, the WHYOS disciples drink toasts to:

Soldier John Kelly
Little Mary Kelly

The Fort of No Return
AND
You Can't Tame a Dead Rabbit

Kidd speaks aloud to his fellow Irish in The Morgue Saloon. "My heart now lies in the Western Frontier, boys, but New York City owns my soul."

The stories of vengeance by the Kellys so impress the WHYOS gang captains that they issue a decree to the effect that an Irishman must first kill a man before becoming a full-fledged member. They use the Irish proverb:

"An Irishman ain't tough until he has knocked his man out."

Kidd and Jack are invited in unanimously to be WHYOS gang members and obtain the tattoo WHYOS on their arms, to supplement their other three. For the next several years, Kidd and Black Jack roam with other WHYOS, but avoid any trouble with the law of New York. Custer cash is ample for any type provisions, with no need for the two Kellys to engage in any criminal activity. They spend their time fishing, hunting, horserace gambling and doing the city nightlife. But as criminal gang life goes, nothing is permanent. Gun battles are prevalent among Irish gangsters seeking control of the operations in the Lower East Side of New York City. Just as in the western towns of Dodge City, Abilene and Tombstone, one hood gunman of New York City calls out another for a pistol duel, "to settle who's boss" and "let the quickest man rule".

Kolleen Kelly's sweetheart, Danny-Boy, is challenged by another Irish hooligan tagged "Saint Joseph". The gun battle to the death is scheduled for high noon. Joseph was given the nickname *Saint* by fellow Irishmen, for his practice of having his prostitutes trade their wares on the corners of the Five Point intersection, while camouflaged as Catholic nuns.

At the request of sister Kolleen, Kidd Kelly lends his military mind to the strategy of Danny-Boy's defense. Danny-Boy's adversary, Saint Joseph, is known to be quick and deadly with a small caliber revolver that he chooses over larger caliber ones for more accuracy. It is reported that Joseph regularly wears some sort of bulletproof vest. To counter St. Joe's tactics, Kidd fashions Danny-Boy a make-shift vest out of what material is available – a pot-belly stove. For a weapon of deadly proportions, Kidd lends Danny one of Absaroka Dapiek's Colt Dragoon .44 caliber revolvers

that Kidd had traded an Army issue Colt .45 Peacemaker for. The massive
Dragoon is the most powerful handgun at that time. The 4 pound 9 ounce
weapon is as effective as a rifle at 100 yards. Kidd instructs Danny not
to get too close to his rival and to use both hands when carefully aiming
the Dragoon. If Danny-Boy shoots St. Joe's torso, only one shot will be
necessary.

As Kidd hands over the Dragoon revolver to Danny-Boy, Danny notices
and reads aloud an inscription that the "liver-eater" had engraved into the
long barrel of the Colt for inspiration, just before he single handedly took
on the whole Crow Indian Nation.

> Fear no enemy of any size
> Just call on me and I will equalize.

The high noon showdown between the two Irish gangsters takes place in
the middle of Paradise Square, at the Five Points intersection. As expected,
St. Joe gets off the first shot, but becomes surprised when Danny-Boy does
not go down when Joe's bullet hits Danny's chest. Suspecting that Danny
may also be wearing a bulletproof vest, Joe quickly fires a second shot at
Danny-Boy's head. But with the human head being a smaller target and
Danny following Kidd's advice to keep a good distance, Joe's second pop
goes astray. In the meantime, Danny has slowly taken aim with the heavy
Dragoon and fires one shot.

50 grains of black powder explode inside the cylinder chamber of
the Dragoon, catapulting a 219-grain bullet at 1500 feet per second, to
penetrate St. Joe's metal vest and turn it to shrapnel.

The Dragoon's blast reverberates off the city's buildings as St. Joe ricochets
down the concrete pavement. Saint Joseph fatally learns that it doesn't
pay to come in second place in a two-man pistol duel.

The noonday gunfight to the death is witnessed by many enjoying their
lunch in the summer sun. In fact, too many, as some happen to be New
York City policemen having their lunch. And they are in a frenzy. The
stray bullet of St. Joe's second shot at Danny-Boy had passed through a
pasty sweet roll that had been in the hands of a police officer, blasting out
the red strawberry preserves that was in the roll, all over the cop. It looks
as if the policeman has been shot. On many occasions the police would
look the other way to gangsters killing gangsters, but not when it comes
down to one of their own going down all police personnel on the scene

abandon their lunch to pounce on Danny-Boy. Danny-Boy is corralled and taken into custody. Even though it becomes clear that the policeman was not shot, Danny is still charged with the murder of Saint Joseph. But because the red preserves that was blown all over the lunching policeman had created panic, the New York City Police Commissioner decrees a "cop commandment".

"When taking a coffee break, all police personnel shall choose donuts to eat rather than pasty sweet rolls. For the donut provides a hole for the passage of stray bullets."

But it is no joke when Danny-Boy goes to trial for the murder of Saint Joe. Even though he pleads self-defense, he is found guilty and sentenced to hang in the Tombs Prison. The trial judge's last words to Danny-Boy are "New York City ain't no Tombstone, Arizona."

The execution of Danny-Boy fuels Kidd's thinking about ending the several-year vacation in New York and returning west where the air is more lead free. For even though many pistol duelers' bullets zip through the skies of the western mining and cow towns during this decade of the 1880's, they are no match for the hundreds of lead UFO's heard flying down the streets of New York City.

Kidd's notion to depart turns to reality when his favorite Broadway Belladonna, Maggie McQuire, with her black hair to match Willowee's, runs a kitchen knife through the throat of another Five Points filly. Kidd and Black Jack are returning west and taking Maggie along to keep her from becoming a Tombs Prison statistic.

Kidd's sister Kolleen also wants out of New York but her sights are aimed towards her homeland of Ireland, where her and brother Kidd's mother is buried. Kidd and Jack, still in possession of much Custer cash, load the purses of Kolleen and other Kelly girls wanting to return to Ireland. Kidd and Jack see the girls off at the ocean dock as Kolleen speaks her final words to brother and nephew. "May the good Lord take a likin' to you boys, but not *too* soon."

Kidd, Black Jack and Maggie board a train going west, where they will split up and go separate ways, once they arrive in St. Louis, Missouri. Black Jack purchases a horse in St. Louis to make an attempt to track down Ed Kelly, who had come to Missouri those years ago, to be near the Younger brothers.

Kidd, knowing the Younger and Jesse James gangs were now out of existence, tries to give his nephew the usual elderly advice. "Watch your back, Jack. It seems that wherever Ed goes, calamity follows," Kidd says in referring to Billy the Kid and Jesse James being gunned down once Ed Kelly paid them a visit.

"Ah, look who's talkin'," is Jack's response. "If Ed's leadin' a curse, you, Uncle are ridin' a reaper."

"Maybe so," Kidd answers. "But I'm your great uncle who covers your ass. Just make sure you write me in Deadwood, on your doin's."

Kidd and Maggie travel on to Kansas, City, where they catch a riverboat steaming up the Missouri River, to eventually skirt their way to Deadwood.

CHAPTER TWENTY THREE
GHOST DANCE

Thanksgiving Day in the month of November 1890, sees Kidd Kelly and Maggie holing up in a miner's shack just off Main Street, Deadwood. For the past two years since they arrived in town, the pair has been living off Kidd's meager Army pension checks and what was left of any Custer cash he brought back from New York. Kidd's leg wound from the Civil War has been giving him hell, making it impossible to do any more scratching for gold nuggets. Maggie has been plying her trade on the streets of Deadwood for extra income. Kidd had won a turkey in a poker game last night and feels kind enough to give his roommate the day off so she may prepare the bird for holiday consumption.

While Maggie toils at the wood-burning stove in their cabin, Kidd drinks alone in a local saloon while waitingfor dinner. He stands at the bar while staring at his own reflection in the mirror on the wall behind the bar. He notices the wrinkles on his face that look as if they have been etched out with a hatchet. His fifty years of life look more like ninety, well pickled from many years of alcohol. His hair is no longer blond, but gray and pulled back in a ponytail. Kidd points a finger at his own image, while talking aloud and not caring who listens.

"You, Kidd Kelly, have taken over the role of the Deadwood Duffer. Deadwood is the perfect tag for what you have become: DEAD WOOD! Wild Bill Hickok may have held the Deadman's Hand, but the bastard's ghost has you playing it out."

Kidd ends his lecture to himself as he slams his shot glass of rot-gut whiskey into the spittoon at his feet. He charges out of the saloon to rejoin Maggie at their cabin. The two are enjoying their Thanksgiving feast of bird and wine when there is a hard knock on the only door in their one room palace with a path to the bath. Kidd opens the door to three unknown men all wearing identical heavy fur-trimmed buckskin coats. The men stand tall in high top black boots, the likes of Cavalry boots. The man who seems to be in charge of the trio requests to speak privately to the man of the house, if he is the one called Kidd Kelly. Kidd does not say a word and clutches the handle of his Colt .45 that sits in his hip holster. He fears a possible ambush. But one of the three tall men, sensing Kidd's uneasiness, quickly pulls back the right sleeve of his coat, exposing a tattoo of a skull over crossed Cavalry sabers, with a green number seven. Kidd's caution turns to curiosity as he relaxes his grip on his revolver. He gives a nod of acknowledgement to the men and snatches his coat off the door hook. Kidd joins the men on a stroll downtown and he takes them to a local saloon that has private curtain closing booths.

The four men settle in and the man who Kidd senses is the leader orders a bottle of the best champagne with four glasses. He requests to Kidd to view his tattoo and becomes surprised to observe that Kidd sports four. The other two men at the table display their 7ᵗʰ Cavalry Avenger tattoos. These three Avengers at the table with Kidd were anxious to meet the man who they heard was the Irishman from New York that originated the 7ᵗʰ Cavalry Avengers. The leader fills Kidd in as to what has occurred in the many years since Kidd retired from U.S. Army life. General Phil Sheridan had passed away two years earlier, in 1888, without having the pleasure to live long enough to toast to the riddance of his other Sioux Indian adversary, Chief Sitting Bull. Sitting Bull had been coaxed by Buffalo Bill Cody, to join Bill's Wild West Show and travel throughout the U.S.A. and countries overseas. Buffalo Bill proclaimed Sitting Bull "The Slayer of George Custer". A total falsehood, but just the same, the remark has infuriated the Custer Avengers. So irritated are some that they wish to personally extinguish the Sioux Chief and give this Buffalo Bill a real Wild West Show! But Sitting Bull has a knack for foreseeing his future and either he tasted vengeance in the wind or Buffalo Bill, who had once warned Wild Bill Hickok of rabid Irishmen pursuing him, may have advised Sitting Bull of the Custer Avengers. Whatever the signal, Sitting Bull and his followers made tracks to Canada, thinking they would be safe from retaliation. However, the U.S. Army put pressure on the Canadians to force Sitting Bull back into the Unites States' jurisdiction with the statement, "If you English boys up North cherish red dog renegades, we'll send you the whole damn lot of 'em!" The Canadians got the picture and escorted Sitting Bull and his clan back south. The lead Custer Avenger tells Kidd that they now have a government-blessed order to "tree 'im".

Sitting Bull has started a religious movement among the Sioux, called *the ghost dance*. It is a belief that Jesus Christ is going to return to Earth as an Indian and run the white man off their land. The Sioux had been preached the story of Jesus Christ through missionary white men. This belief that is circulating throughout the Indian territories is causing great concern among the leaders of white men's churches. The church leaders have put pressure on the U.S. Government to stop this ghost dance nonsense before it gets out of hand. For Indians cannot twist the true meaning of Jesus Christ's return to Earth.

The Custer Avengers are given the opportunity at eliminating the ghost dance movement with the thinking that to extinguish Sitting Bull will put an end to the problem. However, the Custer Avengers want more than just Sitting Bull—they want his whole family. The Avengers had first thought that George Custer might have committed suicide after being shot in the chest because he also had that bullet in his head. The Avengers knew that George had always told his men to keep their last bullet for themselves. Suicide is what the interrogated Sioux Indians said after the battle. Some Avengers become suspicious, though, because George Custer never really expected defeat. After Crow Indian scouts of Custer's 7th Cavalry came forward as to what they witnessed, the Avengers realized that George Custer had actually been assassinated.

Crow Indians were scouting for the 7th Cavalry prior to the Little Big Horn Battle. But when going into the fight, George Custer noticed that his Crow Scouts had removed their cavalry shirts and applied Indian war paint to their skin. This had upset Lt. Colonel Custer, so he dismissed them. The Crow Indian scouts then observed the battle from a distance, with their U.S. Army telescopes. They saw that George was only wounded and unable to continue the fight—but he was still alive. When the battle was over and won by the Indians, George was forced to watch the desecration and mutilation of his wounded men by Indian women and children. The Indian women then jammed sharp wooden sewing awls into his ears while he was still alive. George Custer was then shot in his head, with his own revolver, by Indian Chief Crazy Horse. Hearing all of this from the Crow Indians so infuriates the U.S. Army that more soldiers want in at being Custer Avengers.

Knowing Kidd Kelly had lost many close buddies at Little Big Horn, these three men who had come to Deadwood to locate an original 7th Cavalry Irish Avenger invite Kidd in on the hunt. It is the shot in the dark that Kidd Kelly has been hoping for, to end his useless life about Deadwood. Another shot at glory. Kidd quickly agrees to the three men's offer, so all four of the 7th Cavalry Avengers grasp hands together across the table in the booth. The saloon barmaid, who is in the process of bringing the men another bottle of champagne, stops in her tracks to gawk at the men's tattooed right forearms that pinwheel the table top in a four man handshake.

Kidd returns to this miner's shack, to inform Maggie of his departing for a while. He gives her a kiss goodbye and the remainder of some cash that he had socked away. She gives Kidd the turkey wishbone as a sign of good luck. Kidd grabs what gear he needs and rides out of Deadwood with the three archangels that had come to rescue him.

The month of December sees the U.S. Army initiating their plot to wipe out the ghost dance: **Destroy the leader and you destroy the problem**.

But the Custer Avengers are not to make the elimination of Sitting Bull look like a U.S. Army action. Knowing that Sitting Bull had once had a vision that a bird had come to him to warn him that he would die at the hands of his own people, the Avengers decide to let history record that Chief Sitting Bull was a great prophet. The U.S. Army orders the Indian Police to arrest Sitting Bull. Indian Police are Indians, under the command of the U.S. Army, who get to wear uniforms and nice shiny badges. The leader of the Indian Police is Lieutenant Bull Head. Second in command is an Indian named Red Tomahawk. Red Tomahawk is told by the Custer Avengers that if Sitting Bull is *not* brought in alive, he would become a Lieutenant himself and get to lead his own command of Indian Police. The day the Indian Police go to arrest Sitting Bull at his cabin near Standing Rock, they are followed by a troop of regular Army soldiers sent along just to observe. The Indian Police surround Sitting Bulls cabin, while the U.S. regulars do their observing from a hill nearby.

Lt. Bull Head shouts out an order for Sitting Bull and his followers to come out of the cabin, for they are under arrest. The Indians in the cabin come out all right, but they're comin' a shootin'. Lt. Bull Head is the first to go down and then a few more Indian Police are shot from their horses. Watching the shootout from the hill, the commander of the regular U.S. Army soldiers, orders his sharp shooters to, "pick off Sitting Bull's braves before the whole damned lot of Indian Police get wiped out". The sharp shooters hit their targets in time to save most of the police. As the regulars, with Custer Avengers including Kidd Kelly, ride down to the cabin, they observe that Sitting Bull is on his knees praying a death chant. Indian Policeman Red Tomahawk has the Chief guarded as two other Indian Police bring a young Sioux brave out of the cabin. They force the young Indian to kneel down next to Sitting Bull. The Indian Police inform the regulars that this is Crowfoot, son of Sitting Bull. Custer Avenger, Kidd Kelly, reaches down and picks up the .45 Colt revolver that lays next to Sitting Bull. The revolver has all six cartridges spent.

"Is this one of Custer's men's pieces?" Kidd questions Sitting Bull.

Sitting Bull keeps on praying in his Sioux language without answering Kidd, who is now reloading the revolver with his own .45 caliber ammunition.

"Is it true that your Sioux only wounded George Custer and made *him* watch his wounded men get scalped and mutilated while your squaws drove sticks into his ears?" Kidd growls.

Sitting Bull, who speaks English well, now stops his praying to answer the Avengers. "Custer needs to hear the Indian ways better, in his next life."

"OH YEAH!" The now blood thirsty Kidd snaps. "Did ya then shoot him in the head like this?" Kidd cracks as he puts the revolver that he took from Sitting Bull, to the back of Crowfoots head. Firing one shot, Kidd blasts the young brave's brains out through his eye sockets. Sitting Bull throws himself over his son's dead body and cries aloud in Sioux prayer.

"You're gonna die knowing it was your gun that killed your own son," Kidd says. "And now I'm gonna make your dream come true that you will die by the hands of your own people. Clean his ears out, Red Tomahawk, so he too can hear better in his next life!"

Indian Policeman, Red Tomahawk, who happens to be Sioux, puts the barrel of his rifle to Sitting Bulls ear. Firing one shot, he blasts a hole clean through Sitting Bulls skull, exiting out of his other ear. Over a dozen dead Indians now lay on the ground about the cabin, some police, with as many of Sitting Bulls followers. There is some grumbling among the Indian Police that the soldier sharpshooter had shot some of them.

But the U.S. Army's view is "them damned police would of got wiped out by an ol' Chief and some young bucks, if it wasn't for the regulars. An' what the hell, all the dead from both sides are just Indians. And any dead Indian is one less to feed or worry about." The U.S. Army's belief that if you eliminate Sitting Bull then you eliminate the ghost dance craze is wrong.

Sioux Chief, Big Foot, takes over the helm and gathers up some 300 Indians at Wounded Knee, South Dakota, on December 25th, to celebrate Jesus Christ's birthday and pray for his return to Earth. With the U.S. Army getting fed up with the steady pressure put on them by politicians and the Church to stop this *ghost dance*, they make a dramatic move. "We will send the damned Sioux, the 7th Cavalry and it's Custer Avengers, and with the odds being on our side that Jesus won't show up at the dance, for his birthday cake, we'll send the Sioux to meet Christ."

The 7th Cavalry arrives at Wounded Knee just after Christmas, to join the 9th cavalry and a company of artillerymen. The day of December 28th is just a day for setting up and these 7th Cavalry blue bellies have not made the mistake that Custer's 7th Cavalry did when going to Little Big Horn to face the Sioux. These soldier boys have brought their Gatlin guns and these new issue Hotchkiss machine guns are capable of firing 500 rounds per minute. The rapid-fire artillery guns are placed in high positions, overlooking and surrounding the Sioux encampment. The weapons are to supplement the cannon brought along that fires cans of shot. The infantry soldiers who are to operate these new machine guns lack any real combat time with the pieces, but they are told by a superior officer, "Men, within a short time, expect some real live target practice with your artillery pieces. These are new weapons designed by Doctor Hotchkiss. The Army needs a good account of their abilities, so to receive additional funding from Congress for more."

The evening of this day sees the 7th Cavalry soldiers gathering around campfires to combat the winter chill. Plenty of liquor is available for anti-freeze—after all, it is the holiday season. One of the three Custer Avengers who had rescued Kidd Kelly from his dilemma of being dead wood in Deadwood, requests the Kidd to give some sort of pep rally speech to the young 7th Cavalry soldiers.

Kidd proudly accepts the offer. He stands before a large gathering of soldiers and takes a good long draw from his tobacco pipe just before he starts in. "Boys, my name's Kidd Kelly, I'm an original 7th Cavalry Irish and Custer Avenger that most of you only heard tell about. We knocked out Wild Bill Hickok and his pal, California Joe, for the gunning down of the 7th's John Kelly, because it's death to those who tread on us. Now your name is the 7th Cavalry. It was the 7th who got treaded on by the Sioux Indians at Little Big Horn and it's the Sioux who now sit here at Wounded Knee.

"When we came upon Little Big Horn that hot sweltering summer day a couple days after the battle, we were greeted with the gut-belchin' stench of 18 ton of stripped, scalped, butchered, sun-blackened, gas-bloated, fly-infested, rottin' disemboweled soldier cadavers. It looked like every two and four-legged predator west of the Missouri River was scavenging for their chunk of the spoils and takin' severed body parts to go.

"Why, we couldn't even identify most of the soldiers or what was left of 'em. We had to put what there was of them into ditches and cover 'em up with anything we could find. It wrenched our guts to know we couldn't give 'em a fittin' funeral. But what could we do? We didn't have enough shovels or time to dig some near 250 graves with warring Indians still around. And we sure couldn't load up some 18 ton of quartered decaying soldiers and haul 'em back to the fort.

"Now, you boys remember well your name, and these here Indians' name, when you crawl under your 7th Cavalry blanket tonight. You recall it come sun-up, when you tug on those 7th Cavalry boots and strap 7th Cavalry saddles onto 7th Cavalry horses. And keep it in your guts to what Sioux men, women and children did to Custer's men, especially the wounded, when you sight in these here Sioux with your 7th Cavalry carbines, revolvers and saber. And don't even think for a New York minute that these here Sioux women and children wouldn't like to hack off your privates and stuff 'em in your mouth, just as red dog women and children did to Custer's dead and wounded."

Kidd Kelly ends his speech by handing out some papers for the soldiers to circulate. The papers are crude drawings by an Indian Chief, Red Horse, of his recollection of the battle of Little Big Horn. The drawings that were confiscated from the Chief by Custer Avengers, display dead soldiers with heads and limbs severed off. Kidd Kelly now walks off as another Custer Avenger, who is an active officer of this 7th Cavalry, takes his place.

"Men, and I say MEN because that's what you're going to make of yourselves come tomorrow. In a few days we start a new year, 1891. The folks in Washington want it etched in history that the 1889's was the last decade of the Sioux Indian Nation. Why, they're up there now in the Big House, polishing up Medals of Honor for the soldiers who put on the best show here tomorrow, and get back the great fightin' name of the 7th Cavalry. That's all I got to say...the rest is up to you."

The pep rally sermons by Kidd Kelly and the other Custer Avenger have the soldiers of the 7th all torqued up this night, as they sit around campfires while still enjoying holiday spirits of the drinkable kind. A soldier passes around the drawings by Sioux Chief Red Horse, to those who haven't seen them as yet. The pictographs displaying quartered soldiers at Little Big

Horn only fuel on the rage that fester in the soldiers, as they use sharpening stones to hone their Cavalry sabers to a fine edge. The sharper the blade, the quicker the guillotine, is the cry of the night. Unlike Custer's men, these 7th Cavalry pony soldiers have brought their sabers to the match. And they fully intend to put them to use. Custer Avengers bring out a homemade battle flag that bears the skull, saber and number seven, to match their tattoos. They perform a ritual of cutting themselves superficially, so to wipe their blood on this flag.

An Avenger shouts an ordinance, "Come tomorrow, we will clean off the blood of the 7th from this flag WITH THE BLOOD OF THE SIOUX!"

December 29th's first light shows many 7th Cavalry soldiers still intoxicated, with some not getting any sleep overnight from being too fired up for this day. Soldiers on horseback circle the awakening Indian, to keep them corralled within the reaches of the Army's Hotchkiss machine guns. This day is to be a red buffalo shoot in honor of the departed General Phil Sheridan. As the Sioux mill about after sun-up, the Army soldiers become impatient for some kind of action.

A tall blonde haired soldier of German descent hollers at Kidd Kelly, who he sees milling about with the three Avengers who had brought him here. "Hey, Irishman," the German shouts aloud, "you were prickin' us all night to get even with the Sioux. Ya got us all fired up, so what ya gonna do to get something movin'?"

Kidd requests to one of the other Avengers, to lend him a pair of Cavalry gloves, with the remark to the German. "I'll show you boys how to get a war goin'."

With three Avengers at his side, Kidd Kelly walks down to the congregating Indians, to confront the Sioux Chief Big Foot. Kidd demands to Big Foot, "I'll be takin' your weapon," referring to the Chief's pistol that he has tucked in an Indian embroidered sash about his waist. Big Foot steadfastly refuses, so Kidd slaps the Chief's face with the borrowed Cavalry gloves. Kidd knows this action of humiliation will spark retaliation and what transpires is just what the 7th Cavalry has been hoping for. A young Sioux brave standing near Big Foot and offended by Kidd's action draws his old cap and ball revolver, to fire it at Kidd Kelly. The weakly charged bullet only creases Kidd Kelly's thick buffalo hide coat, but the Indian's shot throws open the door that releases the Army juggernaut.

Hotchkiss machine guns, cannon and soldier hand-held carbines open up with such velocity that within seconds the atmosphere is raining Sioux Indian body parts. Within just one minute, cannon firing canisters full of shot, Hotchkiss machine guns firing 500 rounds each and some 300 Army riflemen, will provide enough firepower to dish out to each and every Sioux that is in attendance at the table, a 4 ounce serving of lead grits for the morning meal. Henceforth, this becomes the initiation of the term, "Have a quarter pounder for breakfast".

The intent of this 7th Cavalry is to completely annihilate the entire Sioux Tribe to match what happened to Custer's 7th. But the liquored up soldiers are shooting some of their own men in erratic crossfire. The inexperienced artillery operators are going wild. The heavy artillery fire is ordered to halt by screaming U.S. officers before they lose too many soldiers to their own careless gunfire. The Cavalry soldiers are ordered to mount their horses, ride down any survivors of the easy picking and finish them off with revolver or saber. One Cavalry soldier will later remark, "When I rode down that Indian boy and lopped off his head with my saber, the kid was running so fast that his headless body kept going until it tripped in a ditch!"

The soldiers only stop their rampage when they become exhausted or their hands begin to cramp from grasping their weapons in the freezing winter air. But some bloodthirsty soldiers continue the carnage by stomping their spurred Cavalry boots into the Sioux Indian skulls.

A blinding snowstorm then begins to set in, threatening a white-out that forces the soldiers to concentrate on quickly gathering up their own casualties.

When the U.S. Army completes the task of retrieving their dead and wounded, a young soldier is heard asking his superior, "Sarge, what about the wounded Indians?"

His Sergeant snaps back, "You can pick up those Sioux who helped Custer's wounded. Let the damned snow bury the rest!"

Only those Indians strong enough to crawl away and catch a loose horse, or bury themselves under other Indian bodies will survive this day, and see the light of the New Year.

January 1st of 1891 rings in the New Year with the 7th Cavalry returning to the carnage scene of Wounded Knee. Hundreds of dead Sioux men, women and children along with horse and dog cadavers, speckle the snow. The snowstorm of December 29th had not lasted long enough to whiten the bloody scene. Many of the Indians lie in ghastly morbid, frozen position, Chief Big Foot being the most notable in his frozen sitting position, with his eyelids still open. Indians who were only wounded had succumbed to the freezing temperature.

Due to most Army soldiers still being too inebriated from celebrating the New Year and their triumphant retaliation victory, civilians have to be hired by the Army and brought along to scoop up the frozen Indian carcasses and toss them on horse-drawn wagons, four bodies high. A large open pit is tediously carved out of the frozen ground, to serve as a burial dumpster. As corpses are dropped into the pit by the civilians, soldiers lineup along the pit's edge while passing among themselves Washington-issued champagne bottles to the victors. They pose for the photographs that are taken by Army photographers. They will forever be seen in their drunken stupor. Two of the soldiers, who are New York gangsters, are holding an armful of rabbit pelts so to put frosting on the Sioux Indian cadavers. The soldiers of the 7th sing their version of Auld Lang Syne:

> **May ol' acquaintance be forgot**
> **When we put you six feet under.**
> **For to tread on the 7th will cause for you**
> **To someday feel our thunder.**

While relishing this occasion, Kidd Kelly notices soldiers gleaning the battlefield of souvenirs left scattered about by the Army's artillery reapers. One soldier is wearing one of the Sioux ghost dance vests that the Indians mistakenly thought bullet proof. The vest has at least a half-dozen bloody holes through it. But the harvesting soldier is also in possession of a large, fine ivory-handled long knife, the likes of the Bowie that Kidd had given to Willowee. Kidd approaches the soldier, so to examine the weapon. After asking the soldier for a look-see, Kidd spots the engraving that Willowee had burnt into the handle, "The knife that cuts both ways".

Kidd trades the soldier a five dollar gold piece for Willowee's knife, as he inquires to where the trooper found it. The soldier points out a body lying face down in the snow. As Kidd hesitantly approaches the corpse, he has to dodge drunken soldiers playing soccer with sabered off frozen Indian heads. They are making bets to see who can kick a head into the pit from the furthest distance. Kidd passes a soldier whom he knows to be an Irish New York WHYOS member, who is plucking out frozen Indian eyeballs with the gang's custom copper thumb talons.

When Kidd finally arrives at the location of the Indian lying face down in the snow, he makes a grim discovery. The body has a noticeable crippled let to match Willowee. He pries the body loose from the frozen turf, to flip it over. Kidd sees that the body is a woman, who had frozen to death with her eyelids still open. The middle-aged woman is Willowee. As Kidd picks up Willowee's frozen body to cradle it in his arms, he stares into her open eyes and is struck with the meaning of those last words that she had spoken to him at the Pine Ridge Reservation those many years ago. *I have had visions that once again I will lie in your powerful arms, looking up into your cougar eyes. But when that day does come, my tongue will no longer speak.*

Kidd cannot allow the woman who taught him the ways of the Indians and had given him years of enjoyment, to be just tossed into some dumpster pit in the ground with others. He knows he must give her a proper burial.

As Kidd walks off the battlefield, while carrying Willowee's body, he is road blocked by a young soldier standing in his path.

"Sir, have you a minute?" The soldier asks. "I heard your rally talk the other night and I thought you might have a few more words of wisdom for me. I'm to put some sort of marker at the Sioux burial site, and I'm hoping you can offer what I should write."

"Damn a marker," Kidd growls, cradling Willowee. "Did the Sioux put up a marker at Little Big Horn for the 7th Cavalry? At least we're burying their 18 tons 'a dead. Now stand aside, boy, I got a real important Indian here that deserves a fittin' funeral."

Kidd commandeers an Army horse drawn wagon and pitches off a few dead frozen Sioux bodies from it. He puts down a blanket to lay Willowee down on it, and drives for the Black Hills in this dead of winter. Willowee had always thought the Black Hills to be sacred grounds. Once there, Kidd finds the ground too frozen for him to dig alone. He locates a cave among the tall pine, and buries her deep inside where the ground is softer. Kidd lays *the knife that cuts both ways* beside her.

Kidd returns to Deadwood to await the coming spring, with hopes that his bad leg will miraculously improve and enable him to return to scratching the creek beds for more Custer gold. In the meanwhile, he continues to live off his pension checks, as Maggie McQuire scratches for gold in miners' pants pockets as she dances the streets of Deadwood.

Indian Policeman Red Tomahawk, Center,
Who Executed Sitting Bull

Indian Policeman Red Tomahawk, Center,
Who Executed Sitting Bull

U.S. Army Machine Gun and Cannon

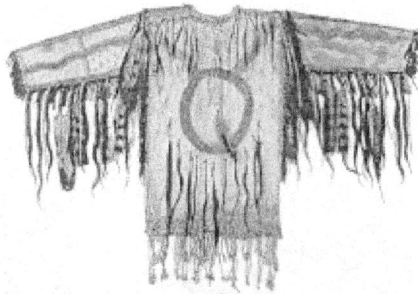

Sioux Indian Ghost Dance Shirts

Sioux Chief Big Foot Frozen Alive

**Indian Red Horses Sketch of Custer's Men at Little Big Horn.
Sketch Infuriated the Custer Avengers**

NOTE: 3rd soldier from right AND left holding rabbit pelts

CHAPTER TWENTY FOUR
FULL FLEDGED WHYOS

As the summer of 1892 approaches the Black Hills of South Dakota, Kidd Kelly comes to the realization that it is the end to his prospecting ways. His old war leg wound just does not want to cooperate.

Kidd has received a letter from nephew Black Jack, stating that Jack and Ed Kelly will be holing up in Creede, Colorado, in this month of June, in hopes of getting in on the mining boom there. Kidd, being bored to death, decides to travel on to Creede, to look up Black Jack and Ed, to see for himself what the action may hold. He again leaves Maggie McQuire to forage for herself as he rides alone.

Once in Creede, Kidd wastes no time in locating Jack and Ed, drinking at a bar in a local saloon. Kidd joins the two and some time into the conversation over beer and whiskey, Jack brings up a matter that Ed has been fuming over.

It seems that Bob Ford, the back shooting killer of Jesse James, has been operating a tent saloon in this here town of Creede, Colorado—and Ed is none too pleased about it.

Kidd inquires, "What's the problem, Ed?"

"Jesse was a friend'a mine," Ed answers. "My auntie married a Younger and the Youngers are kin to the James'."

"Why, Ed," Kidd starts in a pricking demeanor, "that makes you kin to Jesse right enough. But what I have a hard time figuring out is that if Bob Ford gunned down your kin, what's Ford doin' still livin' above ground, and in that there saloon he got with the Missouri Governor's silver that he was givin' for back shootin' Jesse? We Kellys avenge ours, Ed. What ya gonna do, kill Ford in your next life? Ain't no guns in Hell, Ed."

"Ya," Ed flares back, "I've heard all about your New York City Dead Rabbits WHYOS crap."

Black Jack, seeing that Kidd has now gotten Ed riled up, pours Ed more whiskey. "Well, I'll just go call the bastard Ford out in the street and settle up," Ed boasts after downing the shot of booze.

"Call 'im out, hell!" Kidd rambles on. "Ford never gave Jesse a fightin' chance. Back shoot the bastard down like he done Jesse."

Ed Kelly, now fully pushed into high gear by Kidd's jabbing, steps away from the bar to bellow aloud, "I'll show you all some Missouri WHYOS crap. Ya can just get the rabbit ready for Bob Ford's funeral."

Ed charges out the front door of the saloon to grab a shotgun off his horse, before walking down the street towards Ford's saloon.

Kidd comments to Black Jack, once Ed is out of sight, "It's high time for us two ta ride."Kidd and Jack dart out of the saloon and quickly mount their horses. The two point their four legged rides towards the emergency exit of Creede, Colorado.

As they float past the tent saloon that Bob Ford owns and operates, two loud shotgun blasts bulge out the canvas walls."Sounds like Ed's knocked his man out," Black Jack says as he and his uncle urge their horses into a quicker trot.

"Ya," Kidd cracks, "Ed's now a full fledge Missouri WHYOS."

"It was your needlin' that got 'im goin'," Black Jack snaps. "And after these many years a' ridin' alongside you, uncle, I have finally figured out the perfect tag to write your epitaph."

"Now mind your lip, boy," Kidd responds. "You're talkin' 'bout your bad ass uncle, so don't let your tongue cut your throat."

"Ah," Jack exhales before proclaiming his most profound degree. "If Wild Bill Hickok was the Prince of Pistoleers, you, uncle, are without a match the...

King of the Prickaroos!

Kidd Kelly, with nephew Black Jack, travels on for warmer climates, to the Arizona Territory of the west.They settle in Prescott, Arizona to be near kin, Canary Kate Kelly, who spends the remainder of her life, swinging and singing on a rocking chair in the Birdcage Saloon on Whiskey Row.

*Note from the author: I have visited Prescott, Arizona, and located a saloon on Whiskey Row named the Bird Cage. But it is not known by meif it is the same saloon my Grandpa bartended in. However, a boarded up hole in the ceiling can be seen that is easily big enough for a large cage to be lowered down from the second floor.

PROCLAMATION
$5,000⁰⁰
REWARD

FOR EACH of SEVEN ROBBERS of THE TRAIN at WINSTON,MO.,JULY 15,1881, and THE MURDER of CONDUCTER WESTFALL

$ 5,000.00
ADDITIONAL for ARREST or CAPTURE

DEAD OR ALIVE
OF JESSE OR FRANK JAMES

THIS NOTICE TAKES the PLACE of ALL PREVIOUS REWARD NOTICES.

CONTACT SHERIFF, DAVIESS COUNTY, MISSOURI IMMEDIATELY

T. T. CRITTENDEN, GOVERNOR
STATE OF MISSOURI
JULY 26, 1881

Jesse and Frank James' Wanted Poster

Jesse James

Bob Ford With Gun That Killed Jesse

Ed Kelly, Killer of Bob Ford

Courtesy Kansas State Historical Society

Bob Ford's Tent Saloon

The Author's Research

You have read my grandfather's story of the character he met who called himself Kidd Kelly and this Kelly's story. Could it have happened the way this old soldier told it or could he or even my own grandpa have just made up an ol' American West yarn? That's what I wondered well before I took on the task to write it all down. So I read through every book I could locate on the subject of American Old West history in the many libraries I visited. I read a few interesting books but I was finding many contradictions. For example, some authors wrote that Wild Bill Hickok had killed as many as one to five U.S. soldiers of the 7th Cavalry. Some wrote that Hickok killed the soldiers while he was a lawman. Others wrote that the shootings occurred in Paddy Welch's Place, not Tommy Drum's.

Most importantly, I could not locate any books that told of the Bella Union Dance Hall being part of the murder scene of the killing of Wild Bill Hickok—and only one book mentioned the teenage boy witness. To not mention the next-door dance hall and its open archway to the Number Ten Saloon would be the same as to write about the sinking of the Titanic and not mentioning the iceberg.

In order to back up my story of the Dead Rabbits, I decided to go directly to some of the western towns mentioned in this story. I looked through their libraries and museums, hoping to find old newspapers with eyewitness accounts. I indeed found much documented information. Of the many books that I used for my documentation, I did not locate any authors who wrote or even suggested that a Kelly clan was responsible for the killings of the characters in this story. But you will read that this author provides much evidence to support this theory.

Read on, learn the hard facts, find out what the teenage witness said and read my discussion of the many myths that have been written.

Kidd Kelly is the main subject in this story of the Dead Rabbits. Could he be for real? "Kidd" is no doubt a nickname. He could have been any one of the Kelly's listed in the 7th Cavalry role call (see page ___) except for maybe Patrick Kelly, Company I because a soldier "P. Killey" was listed in the 'Tribune Extra' newspaper of Bismark, Dakota, as being killed at Little Big Horn. There were no official 'dog tags', fingerprints or social security numbers during the Civil War. Kidd Kelly could also have spelled his last name O'Kelly, Kelley, Kyle or Kile. If he was a spy for Phil Sheridan's U.S. Army, he may of not even used his real name.

Would the U.S. Army use "top secret" spies out west after the Civil War? I'll answer that with a quote from Major General John Pope, Commander of the Department of the Missouri in a communication to Fort Hays, Kansas:

> I desire therefore to have authentic official reports of Indian or rumored Indian troubles in that region regularly and with this view you are instructed to employ a few reliable men to be kept along the frontier settlements as 'spies' or scouts, to keep you advised constantly. (Custer Come At Once! Page 92)

If Kidd Kelly was a spy and did "dirty work" for the U.S. Army, he would not have used his true name and perhaps never officially existed.

- The Irish gangs of New York City, the Dead Rabbits and WHYOS, can be found in Robert Hash's fine book, *Bloodletters and Badmen*. Nash reports that a Danny Lyon killed another gangster, Joe Quinn in a noonday gun battle in Paradise Square and was hung in The Tombs August 21, 1888. According to Nash, it was Dandy John Dolan who invented the gang's 'eye gougers' that were used to pop out eyeballs. The gougers were worn on the thumbs and Dolan was arrested and hung after Officer Joe Darcy caught Dolan with a victim's eyeballs in his vest pocket. Nash's WHYOS 'hit menu' varies slightly from the one in this book.

- Nash also writes that it was a prostitute named Gentle Maggie who plunged a knife into another prostitute's throat, named Lizzie the Dove. Danny Lyons was their pimp and they fought at his funeral. Lizzie's last words to Maggie were, "I'll meet you in hell and scratch your eyes out there!"

- The all Irish Union Army Regiment, the New York Fighting Sixty-Ninth and its rainbow division can be found in many military and U.S. Civil War encyclopedias.

- The Civil War Almanac reports that nearly 400 women joined the Union Army and Confederate Army respectively during the U.S. Civil War. With no physicals required, the women masqueraded as males.

- The Kelly's are documented in many history books. The Kelly soldiers are listed in Walter Camp's book and that's only the 7th Cavalry. Mr. Camp wrote that he interviewed those soldiers that called themselves "Custer Avengers" but Camp did not disclose their activities.

- Luther S. "Yellowstone" Kelly is featured in an 1877 Harper's Weekly magazine corroborating that he was hired chief scout for the U.S. Army's Cheyenne and Sioux Campaign in 1876. Yellowstone can be found in Time Life's book, *The Scouts*.

- Jack "Black Jack" Kelly is documented by Jack McCall himself when he wrote a letter from his cell in Yankton, South Dakota. This letter was published in the Cheyenne Daily Leader on February 6th 1877.

Dear Friend,

I received your letter and will drop you a few lines to let you know how I am getting along. I am in good health and spirits, hoping that when this reaches you that you will be the same. I have not heard or seen <u>Jack Kelly</u> since I seen you last. McCarty [ed. note: this is McCall's cell mate] is here yet and will get his trial in April. I have got my trial and will be hung Thursday the 1st of March 1877.

I have not heard from any of the boys in the hills. We have had very cold weather here. But comfortable place here. I hope you will get out. You asked me if I thought it would pay to go to the Hills in the spring. I think it would, if you save your money and above all things, let whiskey alone.

So farewell forever on this earth.

Yours,

Jack McCall

This letter by McCall surely proves that he had at least one associate named Kelly in Deadwood.

- Las Vegas, New Mexico police records indicate that "Jack Kelly", Dave Rudabaugh and a few others broke out of the city jail in December of 1881. See: *Bloodletters and Badmen*.

- Jim "Dog" Kelley is documented in Dodge City, Kansas records as being the mayor from 1877 to 1881, when Jim Kenedy shot and killed Dora Hand on October 4th 1878.

- Fanny Wiggins Kelly can be found in Time Life Books. She wrote her book, *Narrative of My Captivity Among the Sioux Indians* in the late 1880s. I never located the book to read it and there are two versions of Mary Kelly's being scalped alive by the Oglala Sioux. A marker for Mary Kelly can be seen on the Old Oregon Trail.

- Billy Kelly of the U.S. Army's 14th Infantry is mentioned in Wild West magazines as the last living witness to the killing of Indian Chief Crazy Horse at Fort Robinson, Nebraska.

- William (Billy) Gentles spent the remainder of his life in the U.S. Army after fleeing New York City. Born in Ireland, he is buried at Fort Douglas.

- Ed O. Kelly is documented in Creede, Colorado police records as killing Bob Ford on June 24th 1892. Santa Fe, New Mexico police records indicate that Ed Kelly was in the city jail with Billy the Kid in May of 1881 just before Billy was killed in the same year by Sheriff Pat Garrett. Source: *Encyclopedias of Lawmen, Outlaws and Gunfighters*.

- John Kelly, the 7th Cavalry soldier whom Wild Bill Hickok shot and killed in Hays City, Kansas, is in Fort Hays Army records as being admitted to the fort's hospital for gunshot wounds received in Hays City July 17th 1870, along with soldier Jeremiah Lanigan. The Topeka, Kansas *Commonwealth* newspaper of July 22nd 1870 states: "Wild Bill Hickok killed a soldier and seriously wounded another."

Sgt. Ryan of the 7th Cavalry, in his memoirs, confirms that Hickok shot Kelly and Lanigan in Tommy Drum's Saloon and not Paddy Welch's Place as some authors wrote. Ryan paints a different picture of how the fight took place, but by his statement, he admits he did not arrive on the scene until John Kelly had breathed his last (Joseph Rosa). Ryan does corroborate that Lanigan later deserted the 7th Cavalry and was killed in Kansas by a soldier named Kelly. There are several writings and Hollywood movies that claim that Marshal Wild Bill Hickok killed several Cavalry soldiers. Let me straighten out this myth. Hickok killed only one soldier, John Kelly, and Hickok was NOT a lawman at the time.

John Kelly had deserted the 7th Cavalry and joined General Carr's 5th Cavalry in early 1869. He went by Kyle and Kile to avoid detection. His reason for deserting Custer's 7th, (as many soldiers did) was because of Custer's harsh treatment of his soldiers. George Custer had a large 15-foot hole dug on the grounds of Fort Hays for a jail stockade. Custer would have unruly soldiers 'hog tied' and put down into this pit. While Kelly was in the 5th Cavalry he was awarded his Congressional Medal of Honor. Quote: "Kyle led his party to a sheltering rock, killed a horse for defense and began to blast away at the Indians, wounding two before the enemy retreated." When Lt. Colonel George Custer heard of John Kelly's award, he wanted Kelly back in the 7th Cavalry.

"The hero belongs to me!" Custer demanded. Kelly returned to the 7th Cavalry. There are no John Kyle's or Kile's listed in the 7th Cavalry, (Walter Camp Notes).

The information on John Kelly can be found in the book, *Custer, Come At Once*.

Joseph G. Rosa, among others, wrote that it was alleged that General Phil Sheridan put out a *Dead or Alive* order to get Hickok after Wild Bill had shot soldiers John Kelly and Jerry Lanigan (*They Called Him Wild Bill* 2nd edition, page 163). General Sheridan would have known that Wild Bill Hickok was not a lawman at the time.

Wild Bill Hickok's documented gunfights are listed in *Encyclopedia of Western Gunfighters*:

1861: July 12th, Rock Creek Station, Nebraska, kills Dave McCanles, James Wood and James Gordon. It's alleged that McCanles is the one who called Hickok, "Duck Bill and a hermaphrodite".

1865: July 21st, Springfield, Missouri, kills Dave Tutt in a street duel.

1869: August 24th, kills John Mulrey while Marshal of Hays City, Kansas.

1869: September 27th, kills Samuel Strawhim while Marshal of Hays City, Kansas.

1870: July 17th, kills 7th Cavalry soldier John Kelly and wounds soldier Jeremiah Lanigan.

1871: October 5th, Abilene, Kansas, Marshal Hickok kills Phil Coe and his own deputy, Mike Williams. Wild Bill had been drinking in the Alamo Saloon when he saw Phil Coe come out the Bulls Head Tavern. Abilene, Kansas records indicate that it was the vigilante group known as the Farmers Protection Association of Dickinson County Kansas who were the ones who drove Wild Bill Hickok out of town after he killed Phil Coe and his own deputy Mike Williams.

- There are many tales as to why Wild Bill Hickok quit or was told to quit Buffalo Bill Cody's Wild West Show. Buffalo Bill wrote that he had to pay Wild Bill's bond in New York City when Hickok hit a cab driver. Joseph Rosa confirms that Wild Bill Hickok did not show up in Deadwood until after Custer's 7th Cavalry was destroyed at Little Big Horn. He showed up with a party that included the Utter brothers, White Eye Anderson, Texas Jack and possibly Calamity Jane.

- The *accurate* description of the Number Ten Saloon and the next-door Bella Union Dance Hall, can be found in Mildred Fielder's book. The Number Ten was located on Lower Main Street, owned by Carl Mann and another named Nutall. The saloon was twenty feet wide and eighty feet long. The bar in the saloon was about eight feet or so long. The next-door Bella Union Dance Hall is described as about twice the size, a typical mining camp theatre, with variety acts, dance stage, gambling games and seventeen curtained boxes facing the stage. There is an open archway between the dance hall and the Number Ten. There is a door in the other side of the dance hall that opens into the Crumbs of Comfort along a crack in the wall. The original Number Ten and Bella Union were hastily and crudely built— and not elaborate as Hollywood movies portray. It is unknown by this writer where the saloon patrons went to urinate. There is confusion to this day (but not by me) about the location of the Number Ten Saloon because it was destroyed in that Deadwood fire of 1879. This confusion starts well before books on Wild Bill Hickok were written, including Joseph G. Rosa's. Pictures of Deadwood just after the fire of 1879, can be seen in the Deadwood museum

- There are writings that when Wild Bill went to the Number Ten on August 2nd, to play cards, he requested the chair with the back to the wall, but Frank Massie would not yield it, so Hickok took the chair across from Massie and had his back to the front or rear door of the saloon.

Impossible! These reports contradict themselves. If Hickok takes the chair across from Massie, then he is facing the wall behind Massie and cannot have his back to any front or rear door of the Number Ten. But then these reports never mention the Bella Union Dance Hall and the open archway. If one does not take in the Bella Union and the archway into any evaluation of the situation that occurred in the Number Ten on August 2ⁿᵈ, 1876, then no conclusion can be accurate. It is surprising to this writer that Joseph G. Rosa never mentioned the Bella Union in his book, *They Called Him Wild Bill.* Some writers claim that Wild Bill Hickok was killed at 4:10 p.m. on August 2ⁿᵈ, 1876. However, the reporter for the Black Hills Pioneer Newspaper printed in his paper that he was on the murder scene just after 3 p.m. I would think that a reporter on the scene would be more accurate than an author not even born yet. There was no official law enforcement of any type in Deadwood at the time when Wild Bill was killed—no sheriff, marshals or police SWAT teams to knock in doors, kick butt, take names and statements from witnesses, gather evidence, recover the murder weapon, have suspects assume the position or draw the chalk-line around Hickok's body. Any joker could have and later did say, "I was there."

- There is some question about where Jack McCall's trial in Deadwood was held. Lucille M. Poznansky, who lived in Deadwood, clears it up: "The Langrishe Company reached Deadwood July 10, 1876. While waiting for a suitable building to be built, Langrishe leased the Bella Union. Right after the Langrishe opening, Wild Bill was killed by Jack McCall in the Number Ten Saloon next door and Langrishe gave the use of the theatre for the Rump court that tried and acquitted McCall." (*Wild Bill and Deadwood* page 104.) As White Eye Anderson said, there was no lousy transcript of McCall's 1ˢᵗ trial.

- Joseph Rosa writes in his book that there was a transcript of Jack McCall's 2ⁿᵈ trial in Yankton, South Dakota. No witness testifies to actually seeing McCall walk up behind Wild Bill and shoot him. They testify to hearing a gunshot and then seeing Jack McCall standing behind Hickok, with a pistol in hand. Frank Massie, who was sitting across from Wild Bill, never noticed McCall until after he heard a gun blast and felt numbness in his arm. Massie had the best seat in the house. If he looks at Wild Bill, he should see who's standing behind him. Massie was either wearing sunglasses or knew more than he told. Witnesses do say that Jack McCall was waving his pistol around to hold back the crowd in the Number Ten. Several say McCall's revolver could not be re-fired and that all ran out before Jack McCall did. (*They Called Him Wild Bill,* 1st and 2nd editions.) Frank Massie stated that he saw Jack McCall on the previous night walk up behind Wild Bill at the card table and pull his pistol. But a young man walked McCall out (1st edition, page 240).Massie never said why he didn't warn Wild Bill of the previous night. Massie didn't know the young man. Was the young man that McCall wrote about in his letter, Jack Kelly, the same? Frank Massie stated that he was carrying around in his arm, the bullet that killed Wild Bill, and that he did not have it removed because it did no permanent damage. Let's take a look at this bucket of testimony that doesn't hold water. The bullet that went through Hickok's head tore out teeth and jawbone according to Ellis Pierce. A slug big enough to rip out bone or teeth is going to be flattened to about the diameter of a dime, as in the 1870's slugs were made of soft lead. A slug near a dime wide is going to make one hell of a tunnel in a human arm when it enters at the wrist and travels to the elbow, as Massie said that the bullet that hit him did. Massie must have had the arms of Bigfoot if he thinks the bullet that hit him is the same that went through Hickok.

Facts:

- The bullet that hit Massie did no permanent damage.

- The bullet that hit Hickok DID do permanent damage.

- The bullet that hit Massie was never removed for its caliber to be identified.

- The murder weapon used to shoot Hickok was NEVER introduced nor its caliber ever proven.

Therefore, Massie's thinking is imaginary. The dictionary describes an imaginary thing "A myth".

Frank Massie, who 'alleged' he was shot
by the same bullet that killed Hickok.

Peter LeFlemme was the teenage boy who was in the Bella Union Dance Hall (which was closed during the daytime) when Wild Bill Hickok was shot in the adjacent Number Ten Saloon. His statement was printed in the Rapid City Journal of November 6th, 1949. LeFlemme states that he was looking out of the front windows when he heard a loud blast that trembled the log walls. **This is very important.** LeFlemme has to be talking about the gun blast percussion trembling the Bella's walls, because that's where he was standing—and we're talking pine log walls. This corroborates that a gunshot or shots were made in the dance hall. LeFlemme goes on by saying that when he heard the gun blast, he fell to the floor in a protective reflex, and did not get up until he heard no more. When he did get up, LeFlemme says that he saw Jack McCall running down Main Street. He then turned to look through the archway that opens into the Number Ten Saloon, where he saw some men attempting to steady Hickok's slumped over body.

Let's look at this part of LeFlemme's statement. Carl Mann, co-owner of the Number Ten Saloon, stated (according to Joseph Rosa) that when Jack McCall tried to fire his revolver five or six times at Hickock's slumped over body and then at the saloon patrons to keep them back, they "all ran out of my house" (i.e. the patrons ran out of the saloon). McCall then made his escape out of the front door. So who were the men that LeFlemme saw around Hickok's slumped over body? And if Pierce says he found Hickok on the floor, were these men really attempting to steady Hickok's body, or were they stabbing it? Peter LeFlemme did not, or could not, identify the men, nor did he ever state why he never mentioned that he was there, until the 1940s.

The characters mentioned in this story as having been in the Number Ten Saloon and the Bella Union Dance Hall when Wild Bill Hickok was killed, are from a combination of testimony at Jack McCall's trial, statements found in Mildred Fielder's book and my grandfather's stories to me.

Peter LeFlemme, when he finally spoke up.

- Jack McCall: now let's take a look at this character and the documented facts about him. McCall used the excuse that he killed Wild Bill because Hickok killed his brother. (*They Called Him Wild Bill,* 1st edition, page 240.) A Mary A. McCall wrote a letter to the Marshal of Yankton, South Dakota when she read that the murderer of Wild Bill was hung. She writes that John "Jack" McCall would be twenty-five years old with light hair and one eye crossed (same description). He has a father, mother and three sisters living in Louisville. There is *no* mention of brothers (*They Called Him Wild Bill,* 2nd edition, pages 347, 348). The Cheyenne Wyoming Daily News of September 1st, 1876 reported that when Jack McCall was held for the killing of Wild Bill Hickok in Deadwood on August 2nd, he had only 43 dollars on his person. The next day, after his release from his first trial in Deadwood, he was seen well dressed, sporting a costly gold watch and displaying a large sum of money. No one has ever explained how or from whom he came across his new-found riches. Was there a plot? When arrested the second time, he's in possession of a .22 caliber pistol that belonged to a U.S. Army soldier. This is not introduced as evidence. After McCall's second trial and while awaiting his hanging, he writes that letter to a friend, from his cell, on January 13, 1877 wondering the whereabouts of "Jack Kelly". Then in February, 1877, he writes to the Yankton Press and Dakotian newspapers to offer an article disclosing the plot to kill Wild Bill Hickok (*They Called Him Wild Bill,* 1st edition, page 242; 2nd edition, page 347). For Governor John Pennington's statement to get McCall pardon see (*They Called Him Wild Bill,* 2nd edition, page 335.) The Daily Press and Dakotian wrote June 23, 1881, that when Jack McCall's body was moved to a new cemetery, his body still had the rope around his neck.

- Since the hanging of Jack McCall, there has been many theories (and I say theories because there is documentation to support them), concerning the plot that McCall had mentioned before he was hung. There are some writings that suggest a man named John Varnes paid McCall to kill Hickok. There are no records to support a John Varnes or any Varnes being in Deadwood or involved in any facet of Wild Bill Hickok's life. "Kelly" is the only name in Deadwood that is synonymous with anyone that Hickok had killed earlier—and Jack McCall is the one who documented it, when he wrote that letter in his cell during January of 1877, to a friend and asking about Kelly.

- There is another rumor that Wild Bill Hickok was killed because the rowdy element of Deadwood feared that he would become the law and clean up the town. Again, we have someone making statements without first checking the facts. Wild Bill was the rowdy element and it was White Eye Anderson who wrote that Hickok camped with them in White Wood Gulch—and Wild Bill never cleaned out or up any town where he was the law. Wild Bill only cleaned up a town by getting himself out of it. Hickok was not the well-liked lawman that dime novels told about or Hollywood movies portray. Hickok lost both sheriff elections he ran in Hays City and Ellsworth, Kansas. Wild Bill was appointed to his lawman positions. When the fine citizens realized Hickok's wild traits, they voted him out of Hays City and ran him out of Abilene.

Sure, Hickok killed three shady characters when he was a lawman. However, those were his personal problems that caused his paranoia to kill his own deputy. Hickok harassed the soldier boys in Hays City and the southern boys in Abilene. No wonder his only trusted friend was a mountain boy. Wild Bill Hickok did not "total" three years as a lawman. In fact, Wild Bill never lasted long in anything he did in life. Sure, maybe a couple of years in the Union Army, but he certainly was not going to desert and face a firing squad. Hickok didn't stay a year scouting for Custer's 7th Cavalry and spent only several months with Buffalo Bill's Wild West Show. Both positions could have led to long employment—well, maybe not Custer's job. When it came to the "settle down with your wife" life, Hickok could only handle that for about four months.

He married Agnes Lake Thatcher, the woman who owned the circus, on March 5, 1876. On the marriage certificate, Hickok wrote that he was 45 years old and that she was 42. This adds fraud to Wild Bill's resume. Agnes was closer to 50 and with Hickok being born on May 27, 1837, and killed on August 2, 1876, he never saw 40 (copy of Hickok's marriage certificate can be seen in the Deadwood Museum).

Yes, Wild Bill Hickok, you might say, was a "Lone Biker". But instead of a motorcycle, he rode a horse. Hickok should have called his horse "Harley". When it looked to Hickok that the coast was clear for him to go to the Black Hills with Custer's 7th wiped out, Wild Bill hopped on his Harley to leave his ol' lady with a warm home of indoor plumbing, hot water, clean linens and square hot meals, just to go shack up in a covered wagon that was the first RV to hit Deadwood, bathe in a cold creek, eat cold tough beef jerky and crap over a log in the weeds and woods of the Black Hills. All so he could have an opportunity to dance with the Deadwood Devil. Maybe this is why every summer the annual motorcycle rally to the Black Hills of South Dakota takes place to commemorate both George Armstrong Custer's and James Butler, Wild Bill Hickok's Run for Glory". But nowadays the Harley riders bring the Ol' Ladies!

Subpoena
Territory of Nebraska
County of Gage

To Monroe McCanles, you are hereby Commanded to appear before me at my Office at Beatrice forthwith to Testify on the part of the Territory against Duck Bill, Dock and Wellman

Dated at Beatrice this 15th day of July AD 1861
T. M. Coulter
Justice of Peace

This subpoena is dated 3 days after Hickok killed Dave McCanles in Nebraska for calling him Duck Bill and a hermaphrodite.

- Colorado Charlie Utter painted a grave headboard for Hickok's burial:

Wild Bill

James B. Hickok

Killed by the Assassin

Jack McCall

In

Deadwood, Black Hills

August 2nd, 1876

PARD

We Will Meet Again

In the Happy

Hunting Ground

To Part No More

Good Bye

Colorado Charlie

C.H. Utter

PARD? Is this short for partner?

Colorado Charlie is the guy who took Wild Bill to meet his Waterloo at the Number Ten Saloon and left him there unguarded, the same day he also sent Wild Bill's only trusted friend, California Joe, out of town (*They Called Him Wild Bill,* 1st edition, page 216). Oh sure, Charlie was nice enough to take control of Hickok's body and fix him up for the funeral, but he was also nice enough to take control of Wild Bill's belongings. What ever happened to Wild Bill's wagon and half-interest in a gold claim he had with Utter, that Agnes Spring wrote about that Wild Bill had in Deadwood? What about his two famed Colt ivory-handled pistols or any other weapons Wild Bill had? Joseph Rosa wrote that Utter buried Wild Bill's carbine with him, but when Wild Bill was dug up in 1879, to be moved to a new cemetery, the carbine wasn't there. Rosa states that he saw Wild Bill's ruby-stubbed gold watch that Charlie Utter sold to an Abilene, Kansas, bartender. What about personal effects such as Wild Bill's smoking pipe and razor that sit in a museum? I am of the opinion that belongings of a deceased belong to the spouse. When Wild Bill's wife, Agnes, came to Deadwood, all she got from Charlie Utter was a long lock of Wild Bill's hair, according to Agnes Spring. And it is said that a lock of Hickok's hair is in the Wilstach Collection of the New York Public Library. I wonder if Wild Bill had any gold fillings. No! Colorado Charlie Utter, you were no pard of Wild Bill Hickok and Hickok knew it himself when he wrote a letter in Deadwood stating that his only trusted friends were his six-gun and California Joe (*They Called Him Wild Bill,* 1st edition, page 295, 2nd edition, page 196). But as you wrote on his tombstone, Charlie, I am pretty damned sure that Wild Bill would have loved to meet up with you again in the happy Hunting Ground. In 1925, it was alleged that the undertaker, Doc Ellis Pierce had stripped Hickok's body and found it covered with knife wounds (*They Called Him Wild Bill,* 2nd edition, page 310-311). Pierce later denied it, stating that he didn't change Hickok's clothes. *But*, the correspondent for the Inter-Ocean, August 17, 1876, reported: "The Corpse was clad in complete dress suit of black broadcloth, New Under Clothing, and white linen shirt, beside him in the coffin lay his trusty rifle." Would Doc Pierce lie about changing Wild Bill's clothes? Let's see. Pierce called himself doc and there is no proof that he ever was a "real" doctor. Pierce admitted to cutting off a chunk of Wild Bill's hair of 14 inches in length (*They Called Him Wild Bill,* 2nd edition, pages 310-311). Pierce quote, "His pistol, Utter, his partner, wished to keep." Do you really think that Wild Bill's trusty rifle is still beside him in his coffin? Doc Pierce and Colorado Charlie Utter were sure nice guys. Agnes W. Springs wrote in her book that Charlie Utter went on to the Panama Canal, called himself a doctor, and sold drugs to the canal construction workers. By the way, Spring also wrote that when Calamity Jane was in Deadwood while Wild Bill was alive, "Calamity laid up with the Utter brothers."

- California Joe's tombstone on the bank of the White River, at Fort Robinson, Nebraska:

Moses Embree Milner
"California Joe"
Born in Stanford, Kentucky
1829
Murdered
October 29, 1876

There are claims that Joe was shot in the back by a man named Tom Newcomb, but this Newcomb was never charged with a crime. These reports also state that Joe was well liked among the soldiers. Who's kidding whom? Yeah, so well liked that a fort full of soldiers would let a back shooter of their friend go free. There was no civilian agency of any type to investigate the killing of a civilian inside of an Army fort out in nowhere. For someone to murder and get away clean, even with witnesses around, it would have to be on their turf. Whose turf is Fort Robinson, Nebraska and who makes out the death certificates? Yeah, the Irishman who has a booze bottle named after his kin – Doctor Valentine T. McGillycuddy.

- U.S. Army records indicate that Oglala Sioux Indian Chief Crazy Horse died in Fort Robinson, Nebraska on September 5, 1877, at the age of 35. The Army corroborates that soldier William Gentles "lanced" the chief in his kidney and although Indians were considered "different", I am pretty sure they were born with two kidneys, just as white men. But then again, this is Sheridan's Army we're talking about. Indians don't write history books and Phil Sheridan, "the only god west of the Mississippi", is credited with being the first to say, "The only good Indian is a dead Indian."

- Time-Life Books indicate that Sioux Indian Chief Sitting Bull, at the age of 59, was shot and killed at his cabin by U.S. Army Indian Police, on December 15, 1890. About eight of his followers, including his son Crowfoot, were also killed. About six or so Indian Police were killed in the fight as U.S. Regulars looked on.

- Time-Life Books detail the Wounded Knee battle (if "battle" is what you want to call it) between U.S. Army soldiers and Sioux Indians. According to Time-Life, most of the 300 or so Indians were killed while about 25 soldiers were killed and 30 wounded. The books contain many pictures of the carnage; the frozen Indians in morbid positions and the pit that they were dumped into. Many soldiers got those Medals of Honor for "Gallant Valor". It is unknown by this author if any Indians received any medals.

- John Johnston, "Liver Eater" is well chronicled in Denis McLaughlin's book. McLaughlin confirms that Johnston was hired by the U.S. Army in 1876 for the Sioux Cheyenne Campaign. Johnston passed away in a California veteran's hospital in January of 1900, at the age of 74. White Eye Anderson wrote that he met Johnston prior to the year of 1876, at the Liver Eater's cabin. They were surrounded by Indians, but Johnston's cabin backed up to a cave for escape purposes, with a tunnel to the other side of the mountain. But before the two men took off through the cave, Johnston baked a batch of biscuits laced with strychnine to leave for the Indians. Anderson further writes that when he went back to the cabin a year later, nearly a dozen Indian skeletons lay around the cabin. White Eye confirms that Liver-eating Johnston did scouting for the U.S. Army, 1876-77, with "Yellowstone", Kelly (*I Buried Hickok,* page 38).

- Hollywood made a movie resembling John Johnston's life called "Jeremiah Johnson", starring Robert Redford. Although Redford must not have had the appetite for liver, he did make the statement to the boy in the movie, "I make damn good biscuits."

- Over 90 percent of the characters in my story of Kidd Kelly can be found in the books mentioned in the back of this book, and or newspapers. That includes Hoodoo Brown, Lottie Deno and even the Hanging Wind Mill (Metz's Encyclopedia).

Now you have seen the historical facts and eyewitness statements that go along with the story of the Kelly clan. You can now see why I had to record these other versions to Old America West history, so others could make their own conclusions. It's a true story that my grandfather told me, of the many stories he said this Kidd Kelly told him over the several years they knew each other—and the evidence I documented is real. Some may think that I could not possibly remember all the details and characters that were in these stories that my grandfather told me years before I wrote them. But there are many men and women that can never forget their experiences during their war years, the names of their buddies and their battles. There are many senior sport fans that can still recite the entire rosters and starting line ups of their favorite sport team of years past (especially Yankee fans). Well it just so happens that MY favorite sport when I was a teenager was, "American Old West Gunfighters and Gangsters". I remember the line-ups, the final scores and the "Hits" and runs. Sure, I embellished the story a bit with the conversations that took place, but it was to enhance the story for the reader. Neither I, nor my grandfather, was alive back in the old west to be able to record any of the characters conversations. But then, who was? So I injected myself into the character of this Kidd Kelly, a confident smart-ass prickaroo gangster from New York City of Irish decent. Someone who had the backing of the only god west of the Mississippi and "his" United States Army, with no civilian law enforcement of any degree to get in his way. But before you form your own opinion on what you have read in this book and if it is true and accurate, I suggest you read what has been written in the books I mention in the back of this book and/or any others you can find on these incidents and their characters. And then re-read this book and make your mind up. Sure, some won't believe it, but then some wouldn't believe it if I told them that water was spelt "H2O".

While searching for evidence to support the versions of history in this book, I came across interesting tales of what may have happened to Wild Bill Hickok's two ivory handled Colt Navy .36 revolvers. Besides other claims to Charlie Storm having one when he was killed in Tombstone, there are writings indicating that Sheriff Pat Garrett used one to kill Billy the Kid. Garrett was later gunned down when he stepped off a horse drawn wagon to urinate along a roadside. If Storm and Garrett had had Hickok's revolvers, then the Kelly's decree ran true: "Wear a dead man's gun and you'll join 'im."

Storm's and Garrett's epitaphs could have read: "Curse of those guns that belonged to the man who was killed when he was dealt, **The Deadman's Hand"**

Author: James Mic Regan

Acknowledgements

City and Police records of:

New York City, New York
Hays City, Kansas
Abilene, Kansas
Dodge City, Kansas
Deadwood, South Dakota
Yankton, South Dakota
Tombstone, Arizona
Santa Fe, New Mexico
Las Vegas, New Mexico
Creede, Colorado

Newspapers:
Tribune Extra, Bismark, D.T.
Clyde Republican Valley Empire
Topeka Kansas Daily Commonwealth
Black Hills Pioneer
Rapid City Daily Journal
Dakotian Press
Cheyenne Daily Leader
Yankton Press
Arizona Republic
Inter-ocean News

U.S. Army records of:
Fort Hays, Kansas
Fort Robinson, Nebraska

Non-fictional books used in my records:

1. *'Blood Letters and Badmen'* by Jay Robert Nash, M. Evans and Company, Inc., New York, New York.
2. *'The Encyclopedia of Lawmen, Outlaws and Gunfighters'* by Leon Claire Metz, Checkmark Books, New York, New York.
3. *'They Called Him Wild Bill'* by Joseph G. Rosa, two editions, Oklahoma Press, Norman, Oklahoma.

4. *'Wild Bill and Deadwood'* by Mildred Fielder, Superior Publishing Company, Seattle, Washington.
5. *'Walter Camp Notes'* by Walter Camp, Brigham Young University Press, Provo, Utah.
6. *'Gun Fighters'* by James D. Horan, Gramercy Books, New York, New York.
7. *'Good Little Bad Man'* by Agnes Wright Springs.
8. *'Encyclopedia of the Old West'* by Denis McLaughlin, Doubleday Books, Garden City, New York.
9. *'Encyclopedia of Western Gunfighters'* by Bill O'Neal, University of Oklahoma Press, Norman, Oklahoma.
10. *'Encyclopedia of Western Lawmen and Outlaws'* by Jay Robert Nash, Paragon House, New York, New York.
11. *'I Buried Hickok'* by William B. Secrest, Creative Publishing Company, College Station, Texas.
12. New York Time Life Books: The Chiefs
                               The Indians
                               The Scouts
                               The Townsmen
13. *'Custer, Come At Once!'* by Blaine Burkey, republished by

Society of Friends of Historic Fort Hays, Hays City, Kansas 1991.

Pictures courtesy of Kansas State Historical Society.

Sketches of Dead Rabbit, 7th Cavalry, Deadman's Hand and Number Ten Bella Union are property of Author James Mic Regan.

Deadwood Daze

The Cavalry found gold in '74
The prospectors in '75,
Painted ladies earned it in '76,
When Custer not alive.

Wild Bill showed in July that year
California Joe by his side,
But Hickok shot in the back and killed
While Joe had took a ride.

Jack McCall caught and sent to court
His charge was the kill,
But jury of miners' love was gold
And not for Wild Bill.

Wild Bill...buried on the hill,
By the man who called him Pard,
But this same man deserted Bill
When he should have been his guard.

Joe went to the Fort of No Return
To call out those who did it,
But he stood alone in the yard that day
And for his answer, came a bullet.

McCall was re-caught and tried again
But this time it's for real,
He tried to talk about the plot
But hung first...lips now sealed.

But some things good must be said
About that Deadman's Hand,
For the first to hold it, then shot down
No doubt the quickest man.

When in a gun duel he had no match
Courage did not lack,
No one dared to face him down

They had to shoot his back.

It's Wild Bill who kissed no ass
Nor ever took one's crap,
He is the reason why Deadwood's now
Forever on the map.

www.ingramcontent.com/pod-product-compliance
Lightning Source LLC
LaVergne TN
LVHW051231080426
835513LV00016B/1525